1 January
Wednesday 2020

I0474897

PRIORITY TASKS		MORNING		AFTERNOON/EVENING
_____	12 AM		12 PM	
_____	1		1	
_____	2		2	
_____	3		3	
_____	4		4	
_____	5		5	
TO DO	6		6	
_____	7		7	
_____	8		8	
_____	9		9	
_____	10		10	
_____	11		11	

NOTES

_____

_____

_____

_____

2

January
Thursday

2020

PRIORITY TASKS

_____

_____

_____

_____

_____

_____

_____

TO DO

_____

_____

_____

_____

_____

_____

_____

_____

NOTES

	MORNING		**AFTERNOON/EVENING**
12 AM		12 PM	
1		1	
2		2	
3		3	
4		4	
5		5	
6		6	
7		7	
8		8	
9		9	
10		10	
11		11	

_____

_____

_____

_____

3

January
Friday

2020

PRIORITY TASKS

	MORNING			AFTERNOON/EVENING
12 AM		12 PM		
1		1		
2		2		
3		3		
4		4		
5		5		
6		6		
7		7		
8		8		
9		9		
10		10		
11		11		

TO DO

NOTES

4

January
Saturday

2020

PRIORITY TASKS

TO DO

NOTES

	MORNING		AFTERNOON/EVENING
12 AM		12 PM	
1		1	
2		2	
3		3	
4		4	
5		5	
6		6	
7		7	
8		8	
9		9	
10		10	
11		11	

5

January
Sunday

2020

PRIORITY TASKS

_____
_____
_____
_____
_____
_____
_____
_____

TO DO

_____
_____
_____
_____
_____
_____
_____

NOTES

	MORNING		AFTERNOON/EVENING
12 AM		12 PM	
1		1	
2		2	
3		3	
4		4	
5		5	
6		6	
7		7	
8		8	
9		9	
10		10	
11		11	

_____
_____
_____
_____

6

January
Monday

2020

PRIORITY TASKS

	MORNING		AFTERNOON/EVENING
12 AM		12 PM	
1		1	
2		2	
3		3	
4		4	
5		5	
6		6	
7		7	
8		8	
9		9	
10		10	
11		11	

TO DO

NOTES

7

January
Tuesday

2020

PRIORITY TASKS

MORNING

AFTERNOON/EVENING

	MORNING		AFTERNOON/EVENING
12 AM		12 PM	
1		1	
2		2	
3		3	
4		4	
5		5	
6		6	
7		7	
8		8	
9		9	
10		10	
11		11	

TO DO

NOTES

8 January **Wednesday** 2020

PRIORITY TASKS

_____

_____

_____

_____

_____

_____

TO DO

_____

_____

_____

_____

_____

_____

NOTES

	MORNING		AFTERNOON/EVENING
12 AM		12 PM	
1		1	
2		2	
3		3	
4		4	
5		5	
6		6	
7		7	
8		8	
9		9	
10		10	
11		11	

_____

_____

_____

_____

9

January
Thursday

2020

PRIORITY TASKS

MORNING

AFTERNOON/EVENING

	MORNING		AFTERNOON/EVENING
12 AM		12 PM	
1		1	
2		2	
3		3	
4		4	
5		5	
6		6	
7		7	
8		8	
9		9	
10		10	
11		11	

TO DO

NOTES

10 January Friday **2020**

MORNING		AFTERNOON/EVENING
12 AM		12 PM
1		1
2		2
3		3
4		4
5		5
6		6
7		7
8		8
9		9
10		10
11		11

TO DO

NOTES

11 January **Saturday** 2020

PRIORITY TASKS

_____
_____
_____
_____
_____
_____
_____

TO DO

_____
_____
_____
_____
_____
_____
_____

NOTES

	MORNING		AFTERNOON/EVENING
12 AM		12 PM	
1		1	
2		2	
3		3	
4		4	
5		5	
6		6	
7		7	
8		8	
9		9	
10		10	
11		11	

_____
_____
_____
_____

12 January
Sunday

2020

PRIORITY TASKS

MORNING		AFTERNOON/EVENING
12 AM		12 PM
1		1
2		2
3		3
4		4
5		5
6		6
7		7
8		8
9		9
10		10
11		11

TO DO

NOTES

13

January
Monday

2020

PRIORITY TASKS

	MORNING		AFTERNOON/EVENING
12 AM		12 PM	
1		1	
2		2	
3		3	
4		4	
5		5	
6		6	
7		7	
8		8	
9		9	
10		10	
11		11	

TO DO

NOTES

14 January
Tuesday

2020

PRIORITY TASKS

MORNING

AFTERNOON/EVENING

	MORNING		AFTERNOON/EVENING
12 AM		12 PM	
1		1	
2		2	
3		3	
4		4	
5		5	
6		6	
7		7	
8		8	
9		9	
10		10	
11		11	

TO DO

NOTES

15 January
Wednesday 2020

PRIORITY TASKS

MORNING

AFTERNOON/EVENING

	MORNING		AFTERNOON/EVENING
12 AM		12 PM	
1		1	
2		2	
3		3	
4		4	
5		5	
6		6	
7		7	
8		8	
9		9	
10		10	
11		11	

TO DO

NOTES

16 January Thursday 2020

PRIORITY TASKS

_____
_____
_____
_____
_____
_____
_____

TO DO

_____
_____
_____
_____
_____
_____
_____

NOTES

MORNING		AFTERNOON/EVENING	
12 AM		12 PM	
1		1	
2		2	
3		3	
4		4	
5		5	
6		6	
7		7	
8		8	
9		9	
10		10	
11		11	

_____
_____
_____
_____

17

January
Friday

2020

PRIORITY TASKS

_____

_____

_____

_____

_____

_____

_____

TO DO

_____

_____

_____

_____

_____

_____

_____

NOTES

MORNING		AFTERNOON/EVENING	
12 AM		12 PM	
1		1	
2		2	
3		3	
4		4	
5		5	
6		6	
7		7	
8		8	
9		9	
10		10	
11		11	

_____

_____

_____

_____

18 January **Saturday** **2020**

MORNING			AFTERNOON/EVENING	
12 AM		12 PM		
1		1		
2		2		
3		3		
4		4		
5		5		
6		6		
7		7		
8		8		
9		9		
10		10		
11		11		

TO DO

NOTES

19 January **Sunday** **2020**

PRIORITY TASKS

	MORNING		AFTERNOON/EVENING
12 AM		12 PM	
1		1	
2		2	
3		3	
4		4	
5		5	
6		6	
7		7	
8		8	
9		9	
10		10	
11		11	

TO DO

NOTES

20 January **Monday** **2020**

	MORNING		AFTERNOON/EVENING
12 AM		12 PM	
1		1	
2		2	
3		3	
4		4	
5		5	
6		6	
7		7	
8		8	
9		9	
10		10	
11		11	

TO DO

NOTES

21 January
Tuesday
2020

PRIORITY TASKS

_____

_____

_____

_____

_____

_____

_____

_____

TO DO

_____

_____

_____

_____

_____

_____

_____

NOTES

MORNING		AFTERNOON/EVENING	
12 AM		12 PM	
1		1	
2		2	
3		3	
4		4	
5		5	
6		6	
7		7	
8		8	
9		9	
10		10	
11		11	

_____

_____

_____

_____

22 January **Wednesday** **2020**

PRIORITY TASKS

_____

_____

_____

_____

_____

_____

TO DO

_____

_____

_____

_____

_____

_____

NOTES

MORNING		AFTERNOON/EVENING	
12 AM		12 PM	
1		1	
2		2	
3		3	
4		4	
5		5	
6		6	
7		7	
8		8	
9		9	
10		10	
11		11	

_____

_____

_____

_____

23 January **Thursday** **2020**

PRIORITY TASKS

_____
_____
_____
_____
_____
_____
_____

TO DO

_____
_____
_____
_____
_____
_____
_____

NOTES

	MORNING		AFTERNOON/EVENING
12 AM		12 PM	
1		1	
2		2	
3		3	
4		4	
5		5	
6		6	
7		7	
8		8	
9		9	
10		10	
11		11	

_____
_____
_____
_____

24 January
Friday

2020

PRIORITY TASKS

MORNING

AFTERNOON/EVENING

	MORNING		AFTERNOON/EVENING
12 AM		12 PM	
1		1	
2		2	
3		3	
4		4	
5		5	
6		6	
7		7	
8		8	
9		9	
10		10	
11		11	

TO DO

NOTES

25 January
Saturday
2020

PRIORITY TASKS

_____
_____
_____
_____
_____
_____
_____

TO DO

_____
_____
_____
_____
_____
_____
_____
_____

NOTES

	MORNING		AFTERNOON/EVENING
12 AM		12 PM	
1		1	
2		2	
3		3	
4		4	
5		5	
6		6	
7		7	
8		8	
9		9	
10		10	
11		11	

_____
_____
_____
_____

26

January
Sunday

2020

PRIORITY TASKS

	MORNING		AFTERNOON/EVENING
12 AM		12 PM	
1		1	
2		2	
3		3	
4		4	
5		5	
6		6	
7		7	
8		8	
9		9	
10		10	
11		11	

TO DO

NOTES

27 January **Monday** **2020**

PRIORITY TASKS

_____
_____
_____
_____
_____
_____
_____

TO DO

_____
_____
_____
_____
_____
_____
_____

NOTES

MORNING		AFTERNOON/EVENING	
12 AM		12 PM	
1		1	
2		2	
3		3	
4		4	
5		5	
6		6	
7		7	
8		8	
9		9	
10		10	
11		11	

_____
_____
_____
_____

28 January **Tuesday** **2020**

	MORNING			AFTERNOON/EVENING
12 AM		12 PM		
1		1		
2		2		
3		3		
4		4		
5		5		
6		6		
7		7		
8		8		
9		9		
10		10		
11		11		

TO DO

NOTES

29 January **Wednesday** **2020**

MORNING   **AFTERNOON/EVENING**

	MORNING		AFTERNOON/EVENING
12 AM		12 PM	
1		1	
2		2	
3		3	
4		4	
5		5	
6		6	
7		7	
8		8	
9		9	
10		10	
11		11	

TO DO

NOTES

30

January
Thursday
2020

PRIORITY TASKS

MORNING

AFTERNOON/EVENING

	MORNING		AFTERNOON/EVENING
12 AM		12 PM	
1		1	
2		2	
3		3	
4		4	
5		5	
6		6	
7		7	
8		8	
9		9	
10		10	
11		11	

TO DO

NOTES

31 January **Friday** 2020

PRIORITY TASKS

_____

_____

_____

_____

_____

_____

TO DO

_____

_____

_____

_____

_____

_____

_____

NOTES

	MORNING		AFTERNOON/EVENING
12 AM		12 PM	
1		1	
2		2	
3		3	
4		4	
5		5	
6		6	
7		7	
8		8	
9		9	
10		10	
11		11	

_____

_____

_____

_____

1 February Saturday 2020

PRIORITY TASKS

_____
_____
_____
_____
_____
_____
_____

TO DO

_____
_____
_____
_____
_____
_____
_____

NOTES

MORNING		AFTERNOON/EVENING	
12 AM		12 PM	
1		1	
2		2	
3		3	
4		4	
5		5	
6		6	
7		7	
8		8	
9		9	
10		10	
11		11	

_____
_____
_____
_____

2 February
Sunday

2020

PRIORITY TASKS

MORNING

AFTERNOON/EVENING

12 AM		12 PM	
1		1	
2		2	
3		3	
4		4	
5		5	
6		6	
7		7	
8		8	
9		9	
10		10	
11		11	

TO DO

NOTES

3 February
Monday

2020

	MORNING		AFTERNOON/EVENING
12 AM		12 PM	
1		1	
2		2	
3		3	
4		4	
5		5	
6		6	
7		7	
8		8	
9		9	
10		10	
11		11	

TO DO

NOTES

4 February **Tuesday** 2020

PRIORITY TASKS

_____
_____
_____
_____
_____
_____
_____

TO DO

_____
_____
_____
_____
_____
_____
_____

NOTES

	MORNING		AFTERNOON/EVENING
12 AM		12 PM	
1		1	
2		2	
3		3	
4		4	
5		5	
6		6	
7		7	
8		8	
9		9	
10		10	
11		11	

_____
_____
_____
_____

5 February **Wednesday** **2020**

	MORNING		AFTERNOON/EVENING
12 AM		12 PM	
1		1	
2		2	
3		3	
4		4	
5		5	
6		6	
7		7	
8		8	
9		9	
10		10	
11		11	

TO DO

NOTES

6
February
Thursday
2020

	MORNING		AFTERNOON/EVENING
12 AM		12 PM	
1		1	
2		2	
3		3	
4		4	
5		5	
6		6	
7		7	
8		8	
9		9	
10		10	
11		11	

TO DO

NOTES

7 February **Friday** **2020**

PRIORITY TASKS

_____
_____
_____
_____
_____
_____
_____

TO DO

_____
_____
_____
_____
_____
_____
_____

NOTES

	MORNING		AFTERNOON/EVENING
12 AM		12 PM	
1		1	
2		2	
3		3	
4		4	
5		5	
6		6	
7		7	
8		8	
9		9	
10		10	
11		11	

_____
_____
_____
_____

8

February
Saturday

2020

PRIORITY TASKS

	MORNING		AFTERNOON/EVENING
12 AM		12 PM	
1		1	
2		2	
3		3	
4		4	
5		5	
6		6	
7		7	
8		8	
9		9	
10		10	
11		11	

TO DO

NOTES

9

February
Sunday

2020

PRIORITY TASKS

MORNING

AFTERNOON/EVENING

12 AM		12 PM	
1		1	
2		2	
3		3	
4		4	
5		5	
6		6	
7		7	
8		8	
9		9	
10		10	
11		11	

TO DO

NOTES

10

February
Monday

2020

PRIORITY TASKS

MORNING		**AFTERNOON/EVENING**

12 AM		12 PM	
1		1	
2		2	
3		3	
4		4	
5		5	
6		6	
7		7	
8		8	
9		9	
10		10	
11		11	

TO DO

NOTES

11 February **Tuesday** **2020**

PRIORITY TASKS

_____
_____
_____
_____
_____
_____
_____

TO DO

_____
_____
_____
_____
_____
_____
_____

NOTES

MORNING		AFTERNOON/EVENING	
12 AM		12 PM	
1		1	
2		2	
3		3	
4		4	
5		5	
6		6	
7		7	
8		8	
9		9	
10		10	
11		11	

_____
_____
_____
_____

12 February
Wednesday 2020

PRIORITY TASKS

_____

_____

_____

_____

_____

_____

TO DO

_____

_____

_____

_____

_____

_____

NOTES

MORNING		AFTERNOON/EVENING	
12 AM		12 PM	
1		1	
2		2	
3		3	
4		4	
5		5	
6		6	
7		7	
8		8	
9		9	
10		10	
11		11	

_____

_____

_____

_____

13

February
Thursday

2020

MORNING

AFTERNOON/EVENING

12 AM		12 PM	
1		1	
2		2	
3		3	
4		4	
5		5	
6		6	
7		7	
8		8	
9		9	
10		10	
11		11	

TO DO

NOTES

14
February
Friday

2020

PRIORITY TASKS

_____

_____

_____

_____

_____

_____

TO DO

_____

_____

_____

_____

_____

_____

NOTES

MORNING		AFTERNOON/EVENING	
12 AM		12 PM	
1		1	
2		2	
3		3	
4		4	
5		5	
6		6	
7		7	
8		8	
9		9	
10		10	
11		11	

_____

_____

_____

_____

15 February Saturday 2020

PRIORITY TASKS

_____
_____
_____
_____
_____
_____
_____

TO DO

_____
_____
_____
_____
_____
_____
_____

NOTES

MORNING		AFTERNOON/EVENING	
12 AM		12 PM	
1		1	
2		2	
3		3	
4		4	
5		5	
6		6	
7		7	
8		8	
9		9	
10		10	
11		11	

_____
_____
_____
_____

16 February Sunday 2020

PRIORITY TASKS

_____

_____

_____

_____

_____

_____

_____

_____

TO DO

_____

_____

_____

_____

_____

_____

_____

_____

NOTES

	MORNING		AFTERNOON/EVENING
12 AM		12 PM	
1		1	
2		2	
3		3	
4		4	
5		5	
6		6	
7		7	
8		8	
9		9	
10		10	
11		11	

_____

_____

_____

_____

17 February Monday 2020

	MORNING		AFTERNOON/EVENING
12 AM		12 PM	
1		1	
2		2	
3		3	
4		4	
5		5	
6		6	
7		7	
8		8	
9		9	
10		10	
11		11	

TO DO

NOTES

18

February
Tuesday

2020

PRIORITY TASKS

MORNING		AFTERNOON/EVENING	
12 AM		12 PM	
1		1	
2		2	
3		3	
4		4	
5		5	
6		6	
7		7	
8		8	
9		9	
10		10	
11		11	

TO DO

NOTES

19 February Wednesday 2020

PRIORITY TASKS

_____
_____
_____
_____
_____
_____
_____
_____

TO DO

_____
_____
_____
_____
_____
_____

NOTES

	MORNING		AFTERNOON/EVENING
12 AM		12 PM	
1		1	
2		2	
3		3	
4		4	
5		5	
6		6	
7		7	
8		8	
9		9	
10		10	
11		11	

_____
_____
_____
_____

20 February **Thursday** 2020

TO DO

NOTES

	MORNING		AFTERNOON/EVENING
12 AM		12 PM	
1		1	
2		2	
3		3	
4		4	
5		5	
6		6	
7		7	
8		8	
9		9	
10		10	
11		11	

21 February Friday   2020

PRIORITY TASKS

_____
_____
_____
_____
_____
_____
_____

TO DO

_____
_____
_____
_____
_____
_____
_____

NOTES

	MORNING		AFTERNOON/EVENING
12 AM		12 PM	
1		1	
2		2	
3		3	
4		4	
5		5	
6		6	
7		7	
8		8	
9		9	
10		10	
11		11	

_____
_____
_____
_____

22 February **Saturday** **2020**

	MORNING		AFTERNOON/EVENING
12 AM		12 PM	
1		1	
2		2	
3		3	
4		4	
5		5	
6		6	
7		7	
8		8	
9		9	
10		10	
11		11	

TO DO

NOTES

23 February Sunday · 2020

PRIORITY TASKS

_____
_____
_____
_____
_____
_____
_____

TO DO

_____
_____
_____
_____
_____
_____
_____

NOTES

	MORNING		AFTERNOON/EVENING
12 AM		12 PM	
1		1	
2		2	
3		3	
4		4	
5		5	
6		6	
7		7	
8		8	
9		9	
10		10	
11		11	

_____
_____
_____
_____

24 February **Monday** **2020**

	MORNING		AFTERNOON/EVENING
12 AM		12 PM	
1		1	
2		2	
3		3	
4		4	
5		5	
6		6	
7		7	
8		8	
9		9	
10		10	
11		11	

TO DO

NOTES

25
February
Tuesday
2020

PRIORITY TASKS

_____

_____

_____

_____

_____

_____

_____

TO DO

_____

_____

_____

_____

_____

_____

_____

_____

NOTES

	MORNING		AFTERNOON/EVENING
12 AM		12 PM	
1		1	
2		2	
3		3	
4		4	
5		5	
6		6	
7		7	
8		8	
9		9	
10		10	
11		11	

_____

_____

_____

_____

26 February Wednesday 2020

PRIORITY TASKS

_____

_____

_____

_____

_____

_____

_____

TO DO

_____

_____

_____

_____

_____

_____

_____

NOTES

	MORNING		AFTERNOON/EVENING
12 AM		12 PM	
1		1	
2		2	
3		3	
4		4	
5		5	
6		6	
7		7	
8		8	
9		9	
10		10	
11		11	

_____

_____

_____

_____

27 February Thursday 2020

PRIORITY TASKS

_____
_____
_____
_____
_____
_____

TO DO

_____
_____
_____
_____
_____
_____

NOTES

MORNING		AFTERNOON/EVENING
12 AM		12 PM
1		1
2		2
3		3
4		4
5		5
6		6
7		7
8		8
9		9
10		10
11		11

_____
_____
_____
_____

28 February
Friday

2020

PRIORITY TASKS

_____
_____
_____
_____
_____
_____
_____

TO DO

_____
_____
_____
_____
_____
_____
_____

NOTES

	MORNING		AFTERNOON/EVENING
12 AM		12 PM	
1		1	
2		2	
3		3	
4		4	
5		5	
6		6	
7		7	
8		8	
9		9	
10		10	
11		11	

_____
_____
_____
_____

29 February **Saturday** **2020**

	MORNING			AFTERNOON/EVENING
12 AM		12 PM		
1		1		
2		2		
3		3		
4		4		
5		5		
6		6		
7		7		
8		8		
9		9		
10		10		
11		11		

TO DO

NOTES

1

March
Sunday

2020

PRIORITY TASKS

MORNING		AFTERNOON/EVENING	
12 AM		12 PM	
1		1	
2		2	
3		3	
4		4	
5		5	
6		6	
7		7	
8		8	
9		9	
10		10	
11		11	

TO DO

NOTES

2

PRIORITY TASKS

	MORNING		AFTERNOON/EVENING
12 AM		12 PM	
1		1	
2		2	
3		3	
4		4	
5		5	
6		6	
7		7	
8		8	
9		9	
10		10	
11		11	

TO DO

NOTES

3

March
Tuesday

2020

PRIORITY TASKS

MORNING

AFTERNOON/EVENING

	MORNING		AFTERNOON/EVENING
12 AM		12 PM	
1		1	
2		2	
3		3	
4		4	
5		5	
6		6	
7		7	
8		8	
9		9	
10		10	
11		11	

TO DO

NOTES

4 March Wednesday 2020

PRIORITY TASKS

_____
_____
_____
_____
_____
_____
_____

TO DO

_____
_____
_____
_____
_____
_____
_____

NOTES

	MORNING		AFTERNOON/EVENING
12 AM		12 PM	
1		1	
2		2	
3		3	
4		4	
5		5	
6		6	
7		7	
8		8	
9		9	
10		10	
11		11	

_____
_____
_____
_____

5

March
Thursday

2020

PRIORITY TASKS

_____

_____

_____

_____

_____

_____

_____

_____

TO DO

_____

_____

_____

_____

_____

_____

_____

_____

NOTES

	MORNING		**AFTERNOON/EVENING**
12 AM		12 PM	
1		1	
2		2	
3		3	
4		4	
5		5	
6		6	
7		7	
8		8	
9		9	
10		10	
11		11	

_____

_____

_____

_____

6 March **Friday** 2020

PRIORITY TASKS

_____
_____
_____
_____
_____
_____
_____
_____

TO DO

_____
_____
_____
_____
_____
_____
_____

NOTES

	MORNING		AFTERNOON/EVENING
12 AM		12 PM	
1		1	
2		2	
3		3	
4		4	
5		5	
6		6	
7		7	
8		8	
9		9	
10		10	
11		11	

_____
_____
_____
_____

7

March
Saturday

2020

PRIORITY TASKS

	MORNING		AFTERNOON/EVENING
12 AM		12 PM	
1		1	
2		2	
3		3	
4		4	
5		5	
6		6	
7		7	
8		8	
9		9	
10		10	
11		11	

TO DO

NOTES

8

March
Sunday

2020

	MORNING		AFTERNOON/EVENING
12 AM		12 PM	
1		1	
2		2	
3		3	
4		4	
5		5	
6		6	
7		7	
8		8	
9		9	
10		10	
11		11	

TO DO

NOTES

9

March
Monday

2020

PRIORITY TASKS

_____

_____

_____

_____

_____

_____

TO DO

_____

_____

_____

_____

_____

_____

NOTES

_____

_____

_____

_____

	MORNING		**AFTERNOON/EVENING**
12 AM		12 PM	
1		1	
2		2	
3		3	
4		4	
5		5	
6		6	
7		7	
8		8	
9		9	
10		10	
11		11	

10 March Tuesday 2020

	MORNING		AFTERNOON/EVENING
12 AM		12 PM	
1		1	
2		2	
3		3	
4		4	
5		5	
6		6	
7		7	
8		8	
9		9	
10		10	
11		11	

TO DO

NOTES

11

PRIORITY TASKS

_____
_____
_____
_____
_____
_____
_____

TO DO

_____
_____
_____
_____
_____
_____
_____

NOTES

MORNING		AFTERNOON/EVENING	
12 AM		12 PM	
1		1	
2		2	
3		3	
4		4	
5		5	
6		6	
7		7	
8		8	
9		9	
10		10	
11		11	

_____
_____
_____
_____

12
March
Thursday
2020

PRIORITY TASKS

MORNING

AFTERNOON/EVENING

12 AM		12 PM	
1		1	
2		2	
3		3	
4		4	
5		5	
6		6	
7		7	
8		8	
9		9	
10		10	
11		11	

TO DO

NOTES

13 March **Friday** 2020

PRIORITY TASKS

_____
_____
_____
_____
_____
_____
_____

TO DO

_____
_____
_____
_____
_____
_____
_____
_____

NOTES

	MORNING		AFTERNOON/EVENING
12 AM		12 PM	
1		1	
2		2	
3		3	
4		4	
5		5	
6		6	
7		7	
8		8	
9		9	
10		10	
11		11	

_____
_____
_____
_____

14 March Saturday   2020

	MORNING		AFTERNOON/EVENING
12 AM		12 PM	
1		1	
2		2	
3		3	
4		4	
5		5	
6		6	
7		7	
8		8	
9		9	
10		10	
11		11	

TO DO

NOTES

15 March **Sunday**

2020

PRIORITY TASKS

_____

_____

_____

_____

_____

_____

TO DO

_____

_____

_____

_____

_____

_____

_____

NOTES

	MORNING		AFTERNOON/EVENING
12 AM		12 PM	
1		1	
2		2	
3		3	
4		4	
5		5	
6		6	
7		7	
8		8	
9		9	
10		10	
11		11	

_____

_____

_____

_____

16
March
Monday

2020

PRIORITY TASKS

12 AM		12 PM	
1		1	
2		2	
3		3	
4		4	
5		5	
6		6	
7		7	
8		8	
9		9	
10		10	
11		11	

TO DO

NOTES

17 March
Tuesday

2020

PRIORITY TASKS

_____

_____

_____

_____

_____

_____

TO DO

_____

_____

_____

_____

_____

_____

NOTES

	MORNING		**AFTERNOON/EVENING**
12 AM		12 PM	
1		1	
2		2	
3		3	
4		4	
5		5	
6		6	
7		7	
8		8	
9		9	
10		10	
11		11	

_____

_____

_____

_____

18 March
Wednesday **2020**

PRIORITY TASKS	MORNING		AFTERNOON/EVENING
	12 AM	12 PM	
	1	1	
	2	2	
	3	3	
	4	4	
	5	5	
TO DO	6	6	
	7	7	
	8	8	
	9	9	
	10	10	
	11	11	

NOTES

19 March Thursday 2020

PRIORITY TASKS

_____
_____
_____
_____
_____
_____
_____

TO DO

_____
_____
_____
_____
_____
_____
_____
_____

NOTES

MORNING		AFTERNOON/EVENING	
12 AM		12 PM	
1		1	
2		2	
3		3	
4		4	
5		5	
6		6	
7		7	
8		8	
9		9	
10		10	
11		11	

_____
_____
_____
_____

20 March Friday   2020

PRIORITY TASKS

_____
_____
_____
_____
_____
_____

TO DO

_____
_____
_____
_____
_____
_____
_____

NOTES

MORNING		AFTERNOON/EVENING
12 AM		12 PM	
1		1	
2		2	
3		3	
4		4	
5		5	
6		6	
7		7	
8		8	
9		9	
10		10	
11		11	

_____
_____
_____
_____

21 March Saturday   2020

PRIORITY TASKS

_____
_____
_____
_____
_____
_____
_____

TO DO

_____
_____
_____
_____
_____
_____
_____
_____

NOTES

	MORNING		AFTERNOON/EVENING
12 AM		12 PM	
1		1	
2		2	
3		3	
4		4	
5		5	
6		6	
7		7	
8		8	
9		9	
10		10	
11		11	

_____
_____
_____
_____

22 March Sunday 2020

	MORNING		AFTERNOON/EVENING
12 AM		12 PM	
1		1	
2		2	
3		3	
4		4	
5		5	
6		6	
7		7	
8		8	
9		9	
10		10	
11		11	

TO DO

NOTES

23

March
Monday

2020

PRIORITY TASKS

	MORNING		AFTERNOON/EVENING
12 AM		12 PM	
1		1	
2		2	
3		3	
4		4	
5		5	
6		6	
7		7	
8		8	
9		9	
10		10	
11		11	

TO DO

NOTES

24 March **Tuesday** 2020

MORNING   **AFTERNOON/EVENING**

	MORNING			AFTERNOON/EVENING
12 AM		12 PM		
1		1		
2		2		
3		3		
4		4		
5		5		
6		6		
7		7		
8		8		
9		9		
10		10		
11		11		

TO DO

NOTES

25

March
Wednesday **2020**

PRIORITY TASKS

	MORNING		AFTERNOON/EVENING
12 AM		12 PM	
1		1	
2		2	
3		3	
4		4	
5		5	
6		6	
7		7	
8		8	
9		9	
10		10	
11		11	

TO DO

NOTES

26 March **Thursday** **2020**

PRIORITY TASKS

MORNING

AFTERNOON/EVENING

12 AM		12 PM
1		1
2		2
3		3
4		4
5		5
6		6
7		7
8		8
9		9
10		10
11		11

TO DO

NOTES

27 March Friday   2020

PRIORITY TASKS

_____
_____
_____
_____
_____
_____
_____

TO DO

_____
_____
_____
_____
_____
_____
_____
_____

NOTES

	MORNING		AFTERNOON/EVENING
12 AM		12 PM	
1		1	
2		2	
3		3	
4		4	
5		5	
6		6	
7		7	
8		8	
9		9	
10		10	
11		11	

_____
_____
_____
_____

28 March Saturday 2020

PRIORITY TASKS

_____
_____
_____
_____
_____
_____
_____
_____

TO DO

_____
_____
_____
_____
_____
_____
_____
_____

NOTES

MORNING		AFTERNOON/EVENING	
12 AM		12 PM	
1		1	
2		2	
3		3	
4		4	
5		5	
6		6	
7		7	
8		8	
9		9	
10		10	
11		11	

_____
_____
_____
_____

29 March Sunday   2020

PRIORITY TASKS

_____
_____
_____
_____
_____
_____
_____
_____

TO DO

_____
_____
_____
_____
_____
_____
_____
_____

NOTES

	MORNING		AFTERNOON/EVENING
12 AM		12 PM	
1		1	
2		2	
3		3	
4		4	
5		5	
6		6	
7		7	
8		8	
9		9	
10		10	
11		11	

_____
_____
_____
_____

30 March Monday 2020

PRIORITY TASKS

_____
_____
_____
_____
_____
_____
_____

TO DO

_____
_____
_____
_____
_____
_____
_____

NOTES

	MORNING		AFTERNOON/EVENING
12 AM		12 PM	
1		1	
2		2	
3		3	
4		4	
5		5	
6		6	
7		7	
8		8	
9		9	
10		10	
11		11	

_____
_____
_____
_____

31 March **Tuesday** **2020**

PRIORITY TASKS

_____
_____
_____
_____
_____
_____
_____
_____

TO DO

_____
_____
_____
_____
_____
_____
_____
_____

NOTES

MORNING		AFTERNOON/EVENING	
12 AM		12 PM	
1		1	
2		2	
3		3	
4		4	
5		5	
6		6	
7		7	
8		8	
9		9	
10		10	
11		11	

_____
_____
_____
_____

1 April
Wednesday **2020**

PRIORITY TASKS

	MORNING		AFTERNOON/EVENING
12 AM		12 PM	
1		1	
2		2	
3		3	
4		4	
5		5	
6		6	
7		7	
8		8	
9		9	
10		10	
11		11	

TO DO

NOTES

2 April
Thursday

2020

PRIORITY TASKS

_____

_____

_____

_____

_____

_____

_____

TO DO

_____

_____

_____

_____

_____

_____

_____

NOTES

	MORNING		AFTERNOON/EVENING
12 AM		12 PM	
1		1	
2		2	
3		3	
4		4	
5		5	
6		6	
7		7	
8		8	
9		9	
10		10	
11		11	

_____

_____

_____

_____

3 April
Friday

2020

PRIORITY TASKS

	MORNING		AFTERNOON/EVENING
12 AM		12 PM	
1		1	
2		2	
3		3	
4		4	
5		5	
6		6	
7		7	
8		8	
9		9	
10		10	
11		11	

TO DO

NOTES

4 April **Saturday** **2020**

	MORNING		AFTERNOON/EVENING
12 AM		12 PM	
1		1	
2		2	
3		3	
4		4	
5		5	
6		6	
7		7	
8		8	
9		9	
10		10	
11		11	

TO DO

NOTES

5 April **Sunday** 2020

PRIORITY TASKS

MORNING

AFTERNOON/EVENING

	MORNING		AFTERNOON/EVENING
12 AM		12 PM	
1		1	
2		2	
3		3	
4		4	
5		5	
6		6	
7		7	
8		8	
9		9	
10		10	
11		11	

TO DO

NOTES

6

April
Monday

2020

PRIORITY TASKS

MORNING

AFTERNOON/EVENING

12 AM		12 PM	
1		1	
2		2	
3		3	
4		4	
5		5	
6		6	
7		7	
8		8	
9		9	
10		10	
11		11	

TO DO

NOTES

7

April
Tuesday

2020

PRIORITY TASKS

_____

_____

_____

_____

_____

_____

TO DO

_____

_____

_____

_____

_____

_____

_____

_____

NOTES

MORNING		AFTERNOON/EVENING
12 AM		12 PM
1		1
2		2
3		3
4		4
5		5
6		6
7		7
8		8
9		9
10		10
11		11

_____

_____

_____

_____

8 April
Wednesday **2020**

PRIORITY TASKS

MORNING | AFTERNOON/EVENING

12 AM		12 PM	
1		1	
2		2	
3		3	
4		4	
5		5	
6		6	
7		7	
8		8	
9		9	
10		10	
11		11	

TO DO

NOTES

9 April **Thursday** **2020**

	MORNING		AFTERNOON/EVENING
12 AM		12 PM	
1		1	
2		2	
3		3	
4		4	
5		5	
6		6	
7		7	
8		8	
9		9	
10		10	
11		11	

TO DO

NOTES

10
April
Friday

2020

PRIORITY TASKS

_____

_____

_____

_____

_____

_____

_____

TO DO

_____

_____

_____

_____

_____

_____

_____

_____

NOTES

MORNING		AFTERNOON/EVENING	
12 AM		12 PM	
1		1	
2		2	
3		3	
4		4	
5		5	
6		6	
7		7	
8		8	
9		9	
10		10	
11		11	

_____

_____

_____

_____

11 April Saturday 2020

PRIORITY TASKS

_____

_____

_____

_____

_____

_____

_____

_____

TO DO

_____

_____

_____

_____

_____

_____

_____

_____

_____

NOTES

MORNING		AFTERNOON/EVENING	
12 AM		12 PM	
1		1	
2		2	
3		3	
4		4	
5		5	
6		6	
7		7	
8		8	
9		9	
10		10	
11		11	

_____

_____

_____

_____

_____

12 April **Sunday** **2020**

PRIORITY TASKS

_____

_____

_____

_____

_____

_____

_____

TO DO

_____

_____

_____

_____

_____

_____

_____

NOTES

	MORNING		AFTERNOON/EVENING
12 AM		12 PM	
1		1	
2		2	
3		3	
4		4	
5		5	
6		6	
7		7	
8		8	
9		9	
10		10	
11		11	

_____

_____

_____

_____

13
April
Monday
2020

PRIORITY TASKS

TO DO

NOTES

	MORNING		AFTERNOON/EVENING
12 AM		12 PM	
1		1	
2		2	
3		3	
4		4	
5		5	
6		6	
7		7	
8		8	
9		9	
10		10	
11		11	

14 April Tuesday 2020

PRIORITY TASKS

_____

_____

_____

_____

_____

_____

TO DO

_____

_____

_____

_____

_____

_____

_____

NOTES

MORNING		AFTERNOON/EVENING	
12 AM		12 PM	
1		1	
2		2	
3		3	
4		4	
5		5	
6		6	
7		7	
8		8	
9		9	
10		10	
11		11	

_____

_____

_____

_____

15 April
Wednesday 2020

PRIORITY TASKS

_____
_____
_____
_____
_____
_____
_____
_____

TO DO

_____
_____
_____
_____
_____
_____
_____

NOTES

	MORNING		AFTERNOON/EVENING
12 AM		12 PM	
1		1	
2		2	
3		3	
4		4	
5		5	
6		6	
7		7	
8		8	
9		9	
10		10	
11		11	

_____
_____
_____
_____

16 April **Thursday** **2020**

	MORNING		AFTERNOON/EVENING
12 AM		12 PM	
1		1	
2		2	
3		3	
4		4	
5		5	
6		6	
7		7	
8		8	
9		9	
10		10	
11		11	

TO DO

NOTES

17

April
Friday

2020

PRIORITY TASKS

	MORNING		AFTERNOON/EVENING
12 AM		12 PM	
1		1	
2		2	
3		3	
4		4	
5		5	
6		6	
7		7	
8		8	
9		9	
10		10	
11		11	

TO DO

NOTES

18
April
Saturday
2020

PRIORITY TASKS

_____

_____

_____

_____

_____

_____

_____

TO DO

_____

_____

_____

_____

_____

_____

_____

NOTES

MORNING		**AFTERNOON/EVENING**	
12 AM		12 PM	
1		1	
2		2	
3		3	
4		4	
5		5	
6		6	
7		7	
8		8	
9		9	
10		10	
11		11	

_____

_____

_____

_____

19 April Sunday 2020

PRIORITY TASKS

_____
_____
_____
_____
_____
_____
_____
_____

TO DO

_____
_____
_____
_____
_____
_____
_____
_____
_____

NOTES

MORNING		AFTERNOON/EVENING	
12 AM		12 PM	
1		1	
2		2	
3		3	
4		4	
5		5	
6		6	
7		7	
8		8	
9		9	
10		10	
11		11	

_____
_____
_____
_____

20
April
Monday
2020

PRIORITY TASKS

_____

_____

_____

_____

_____

_____

TO DO

_____

_____

_____

_____

_____

_____

NOTES

MORNING		AFTERNOON/EVENING
12 AM		12 PM
1		1
2		2
3		3
4		4
5		5
6		6
7		7
8		8
9		9
10		10
11		11

_____

_____

_____

_____

21 April **Tuesday**   **2020**

PRIORITY TASKS

_____

_____

_____

_____

_____

_____

_____

TO DO

_____

_____

_____

_____

_____

_____

_____

NOTES

	MORNING		AFTERNOON/EVENING
12 AM		12 PM	
1		1	
2		2	
3		3	
4		4	
5		5	
6		6	
7		7	
8		8	
9		9	
10		10	
11		11	

_____

_____

_____

_____

22 April
Wednesday **2020**

PRIORITY TASKS

_____
_____
_____
_____
_____
_____
_____

TO DO

_____
_____
_____
_____
_____
_____
_____
_____

NOTES

MORNING		AFTERNOON/EVENING	
12 AM		12 PM	
1		1	
2		2	
3		3	
4		4	
5		5	
6		6	
7		7	
8		8	
9		9	
10		10	
11		11	

_____
_____
_____
_____

23 April Thursday 2020

PRIORITY TASKS

_____
_____
_____
_____
_____
_____
_____

TO DO

_____
_____
_____
_____
_____
_____
_____

NOTES

	MORNING		AFTERNOON/EVENING
12 AM		12 PM	
1		1	
2		2	
3		3	
4		4	
5		5	
6		6	
7		7	
8		8	
9		9	
10		10	
11		11	

_____
_____
_____
_____

24 April Friday   **2020**

PRIORITY TASKS

	MORNING		AFTERNOON/EVENING
12 AM		12 PM	
1		1	
2		2	
3		3	
4		4	
5		5	
6		6	
7		7	
8		8	
9		9	
10		10	
11		11	

TO DO

NOTES

25 April Saturday 2020

	MORNING		AFTERNOON/EVENING
12 AM		12 PM	
1		1	
2		2	
3		3	
4		4	
5		5	
6		6	
7		7	
8		8	
9		9	
10		10	
11		11	

TO DO

NOTES

26 April
Sunday

2020

PRIORITY TASKS

_____

_____

_____

_____

_____

_____

TO DO

_____

_____

_____

_____

_____

_____

_____

NOTES

MORNING		AFTERNOON/EVENING	
12 AM		12 PM	
1		1	
2		2	
3		3	
4		4	
5		5	
6		6	
7		7	
8		8	
9		9	
10		10	
11		11	

_____

_____

_____

_____

27 April **Monday** **2020**

PRIORITY TASKS

	MORNING		AFTERNOON/EVENING
12 AM		12 PM	
1		1	
2		2	
3		3	
4		4	
5		5	
6		6	
7		7	
8		8	
9		9	
10		10	
11		11	

TO DO

NOTES

28 April **Tuesday**   **2020**

PRIORITY TASKS

_____

_____

_____

_____

_____

_____

_____

TO DO

_____

_____

_____

_____

_____

_____

_____

NOTES

MORNING		**AFTERNOON/EVENING**	
12 AM		12 PM	
1		1	
2		2	
3		3	
4		4	
5		5	
6		6	
7		7	
8		8	
9		9	
10		10	
11		11	

_____

_____

_____

_____

29 April Wednesday 2020

PRIORITY TASKS

_____
_____
_____
_____
_____
_____
_____
_____

TO DO

_____
_____
_____
_____
_____
_____
_____
_____

NOTES

	MORNING		AFTERNOON/EVENING
12 AM		12 PM	
1		1	
2		2	
3		3	
4		4	
5		5	
6		6	
7		7	
8		8	
9		9	
10		10	
11		11	

_____
_____
_____
_____

30 April **Thursday** 2020

	MORNING		AFTERNOON/EVENING
12 AM		12 PM	
1		1	
2		2	
3		3	
4		4	
5		5	
6		6	
7		7	
8		8	
9		9	
10		10	
11		11	

TO DO

NOTES

1

May
Friday

2020

MORNING

AFTERNOON/EVENING

	MORNING		AFTERNOON/EVENING
12 AM		12 PM	
1		1	
2		2	
3		3	
4		4	
5		5	
6		6	
7		7	
8		8	
9		9	
10		10	
11		11	

TO DO

NOTES

2 May **Saturday** 2020

PRIORITY TASKS

_____

_____

_____

_____

_____

_____

TO DO

_____

_____

_____

_____

_____

_____

NOTES

	MORNING		AFTERNOON/EVENING
12 AM		12 PM	
1		1	
2		2	
3		3	
4		4	
5		5	
6		6	
7		7	
8		8	
9		9	
10		10	
11		11	

_____

_____

_____

_____

3

May
Sunday

2020

PRIORITY TASKS

MORNING		AFTERNOON/EVENING

TO DO

	MORNING		AFTERNOON/EVENING
12 AM		12 PM	
1		1	
2		2	
3		3	
4		4	
5		5	
6		6	
7		7	
8		8	
9		9	
10		10	
11		11	

NOTES

4 May
Monday **2020**

	MORNING		AFTERNOON/EVENING
12 AM		12 PM	
1		1	
2		2	
3		3	
4		4	
5		5	
6		6	
7		7	
8		8	
9		9	
10		10	
11		11	

TO DO

NOTES

5

May
Tuesday

2020

PRIORITY TASKS

_____

_____

_____

_____

_____

_____

_____

TO DO

_____

_____

_____

_____

_____

_____

NOTES

	MORNING		AFTERNOON/EVENING
12 AM		12 PM	
1		1	
2		2	
3		3	
4		4	
5		5	
6		6	
7		7	
8		8	
9		9	
10		10	
11		11	

_____

_____

_____

_____

6

PRIORITY TASKS

MORNING		AFTERNOON/EVENING	
12 AM		12 PM	
1		1	
2		2	
3		3	
4		4	
5		5	
6		6	
7		7	
8		8	
9		9	
10		10	
11		11	

TO DO

NOTES

7 May
Thursday
2020

PRIORITY TASKS

MORNING

AFTERNOON/EVENING

12 AM		12 PM	
1		1	
2		2	
3		3	
4		4	
5		5	
6		6	
7		7	
8		8	
9		9	
10		10	
11		11	

TO DO

NOTES

8 May **Friday** 2020

PRIORITY TASKS

_____

_____

_____

_____

_____

TO DO

_____

_____

_____

_____

_____

_____

NOTES

	MORNING		AFTERNOON/EVENING
12 AM		12 PM	
1		1	
2		2	
3		3	
4		4	
5		5	
6		6	
7		7	
8		8	
9		9	
10		10	
11		11	

_____

_____

_____

_____

9

May
Saturday

2020

	MORNING		AFTERNOON/EVENING
12 AM		12 PM	
1		1	
2		2	
3		3	
4		4	
5		5	
6		6	
7		7	
8		8	
9		9	
10		10	
11		11	

TO DO

NOTES

10 May Sunday 2020

PRIORITY TASKS

_____
_____
_____
_____
_____
_____
_____

TO DO

_____
_____
_____
_____
_____
_____
_____

NOTES

	MORNING		AFTERNOON/EVENING
12 AM		12 PM	
1		1	
2		2	
3		3	
4		4	
5		5	
6		6	
7		7	
8		8	
9		9	
10		10	
11		11	

_____
_____
_____
_____

11 May Monday 2020

PRIORITY TASKS

_____
_____
_____
_____
_____
_____
_____
_____

TO DO

_____
_____
_____
_____
_____
_____
_____

NOTES

MORNING		AFTERNOON/EVENING	
12 AM		12 PM	
1		1	
2		2	
3		3	
4		4	
5		5	
6		6	
7		7	
8		8	
9		9	
10		10	
11		11	

_____
_____
_____
_____

12 May **Tuesday**   **2020**

	MORNING		AFTERNOON/EVENING
12 AM		12 PM	
1		1	
2		2	
3		3	
4		4	
5		5	
6		6	
7		7	
8		8	
9		9	
10		10	
11		11	

TO DO

NOTES

13 May
Wednesday **2020**

PRIORITY TASKS

_____

_____

_____

_____

_____

_____

TO DO

_____

_____

_____

_____

_____

_____

NOTES

	MORNING		AFTERNOON/EVENING
12 AM		12 PM	
1		1	
2		2	
3		3	
4		4	
5		5	
6		6	
7		7	
8		8	
9		9	
10		10	
11		11	

_____

_____

_____

_____

14 May **Thursday** **2020**

PRIORITY TASKS

_____
_____
_____
_____
_____
_____

TO DO

_____
_____
_____
_____
_____
_____

NOTES

MORNING		AFTERNOON/EVENING	
12 AM		12 PM	
1		1	
2		2	
3		3	
4		4	
5		5	
6		6	
7		7	
8		8	
9		9	
10		10	
11		11	

_____
_____
_____
_____

15 May Friday   2020

	MORNING			AFTERNOON/EVENING
12 AM		12 PM		
1		1		
2		2		
3		3		
4		4		
5		5		
6		6		
7		7		
8		8		
9		9		
10		10		
11		11		

TO DO

NOTES

16

May
Saturday

2020

MORNING

AFTERNOON/EVENING

	MORNING		AFTERNOON/EVENING
12 AM		12 PM	
1		1	
2		2	
3		3	
4		4	
5		5	
6		6	
7		7	
8		8	
9		9	
10		10	
11		11	

TO DO

NOTES

17 May Sunday   2020

PRIORITY TASKS

_____
_____
_____
_____
_____
_____
_____

TO DO

_____
_____
_____
_____
_____
_____
_____

NOTES

MORNING		AFTERNOON/EVENING	
12 AM		12 PM	
1		1	
2		2	
3		3	
4		4	
5		5	
6		6	
7		7	
8		8	
9		9	
10		10	
11		11	

_____
_____
_____
_____

18

May
Monday

2020

PRIORITY TASKS

MORNING		AFTERNOON/EVENING	
12 AM		12 PM	
1		1	
2		2	
3		3	
4		4	
5		5	
6		6	
7		7	
8		8	
9		9	
10		10	
11		11	

TO DO

NOTES

19 May Tuesday 2020

PRIORITY TASKS

_____
_____
_____
_____
_____
_____
_____
_____

TO DO

_____
_____
_____
_____
_____
_____
_____

NOTES

MORNING		AFTERNOON/EVENING	
12 AM		12 PM	
1		1	
2		2	
3		3	
4		4	
5		5	
6		6	
7		7	
8		8	
9		9	
10		10	
11		11	

_____
_____
_____
_____

20 May Wednesday 2020

PRIORITY TASKS

_____
_____
_____
_____
_____
_____
_____

TO DO

_____
_____
_____
_____
_____
_____
_____

NOTES

	MORNING		AFTERNOON/EVENING
12 AM		12 PM	
1		1	
2		2	
3		3	
4		4	
5		5	
6		6	
7		7	
8		8	
9		9	
10		10	
11		11	

_____
_____
_____
_____

21 May Thursday 2020

PRIORITY TASKS

_____
_____
_____
_____
_____
_____
_____

TO DO

_____
_____
_____
_____
_____
_____
_____

NOTES

MORNING		AFTERNOON/EVENING
12 AM	12 PM	
1	1	
2	2	
3	3	
4	4	
5	5	
6	6	
7	7	
8	8	
9	9	
10	10	
11	11	

_____
_____
_____
_____

22 May
Friday

2020

PRIORITY TASKS

_____
_____
_____
_____
_____
_____
_____
_____

TO DO

_____
_____
_____
_____
_____
_____
_____

NOTES

MORNING		AFTERNOON/EVENING	
12 AM		12 PM	
1		1	
2		2	
3		3	
4		4	
5		5	
6		6	
7		7	
8		8	
9		9	
10		10	
11		11	

_____
_____
_____
_____

23 May Saturday 2020

MORNING

AFTERNOON/EVENING

	MORNING		AFTERNOON/EVENING
12 AM		12 PM	
1		1	
2		2	
3		3	
4		4	
5		5	
6		6	
7		7	
8		8	
9		9	
10		10	
11		11	

TO DO

NOTES

24 May Sunday   2020

PRIORITY TASKS

_____
_____
_____
_____
_____
_____
_____
_____

TO DO

_____
_____
_____
_____
_____
_____
_____
_____
_____

NOTES

	MORNING		AFTERNOON/EVENING
12 AM		12 PM	
1		1	
2		2	
3		3	
4		4	
5		5	
6		6	
7		7	
8		8	
9		9	
10		10	
11		11	

_____
_____
_____
_____

25 May Monday 2020

PRIORITY TASKS

_____

_____

_____

_____

_____

_____

_____

TO DO

_____

_____

_____

_____

_____

_____

_____

NOTES

MORNING		AFTERNOON/EVENING	
12 AM		12 PM	
1		1	
2		2	
3		3	
4		4	
5		5	
6		6	
7		7	
8		8	
9		9	
10		10	
11		11	

_____

_____

_____

_____

26 May Tuesday   2020

MORNING		AFTERNOON/EVENING	
12 AM		12 PM	
1		1	
2		2	
3		3	
4		4	
5		5	
6		6	
7		7	
8		8	
9		9	
10		10	
11		11	

TO DO

NOTES

27 May Wednesday 2020

PRIORITY TASKS

_____

_____

_____

_____

_____

_____

_____

TO DO

_____

_____

_____

_____

_____

_____

NOTES

MORNING		AFTERNOON/EVENING	
12 AM		12 PM	
1		1	
2		2	
3		3	
4		4	
5		5	
6		6	
7		7	
8		8	
9		9	
10		10	
11		11	

_____

_____

_____

_____

28 May **Thursday** 2020

PRIORITY TASKS

_____
_____
_____
_____
_____
_____
_____

TO DO

_____
_____
_____
_____
_____
_____
_____
_____

NOTES

	MORNING		AFTERNOON/EVENING
12 AM		12 PM	
1		1	
2		2	
3		3	
4		4	
5		5	
6		6	
7		7	
8		8	
9		9	
10		10	
11		11	

_____
_____
_____
_____

29

May
Friday

2020

PRIORITY TASKS

_____

_____

_____

_____

_____

_____

_____

_____

TO DO

_____

_____

_____

_____

_____

_____

_____

NOTES

	MORNING		AFTERNOON/EVENING
12 AM		12 PM	
1		1	
2		2	
3		3	
4		4	
5		5	
6		6	
7		7	
8		8	
9		9	
10		10	
11		11	

_____

_____

_____

_____

30 May Saturday   2020

	MORNING			AFTERNOON/EVENING
12 AM		12 PM	
1		1	
2		2	
3		3	
4		4	
5		5	
6		6	
7		7	
8		8	
9		9	
10		10	
11		11	

TO DO

NOTES

31 May Sunday   2020

PRIORITY TASKS

_____
_____
_____
_____
_____
_____

TO DO

_____
_____
_____
_____
_____
_____

NOTES

MORNING		AFTERNOON/EVENING
12 AM		12 PM
1		1
2		2
3		3
4		4
5		5
6		6
7		7
8		8
9		9
10		10
11		11

_____
_____
_____
_____

1

June

Monday

2020

PRIORITY TASKS

_____

_____

_____

_____

_____

_____

_____

TO DO

_____

_____

_____

_____

_____

_____

_____

NOTES

	MORNING		AFTERNOON/EVENING
12 AM		12 PM	
1		1	
2		2	
3		3	
4		4	
5		5	
6		6	
7		7	
8		8	
9		9	
10		10	
11		11	

_____

_____

_____

_____

2 June
Tuesday
2020

PRIORITY TASKS

TO DO

NOTES

	MORNING		AFTERNOON/EVENING
12 AM		12 PM	
1		1	
2		2	
3		3	
4		4	
5		5	
6		6	
7		7	
8		8	
9		9	
10		10	
11		11	

3

June
Wednesday   **2020**

PRIORITY TASKS

	MORNING		AFTERNOON/EVENING
12 AM		12 PM	
1		1	
2		2	
3		3	
4		4	
5		5	
6		6	
7		7	
8		8	
9		9	
10		10	
11		11	

TO DO

NOTES

4

June
Thursday

2020

PRIORITY TASKS

MORNING

AFTERNOON/EVENING

12 AM		12 PM	
1		1	
2		2	
3		3	
4		4	
5		5	
6		6	
7		7	
8		8	
9		9	
10		10	
11		11	

TO DO

NOTES

5 June
Friday

2020

PRIORITY TASKS

TO DO

NOTES

	MORNING		AFTERNOON/EVENING
12 AM		12 PM	
1		1	
2		2	
3		3	
4		4	
5		5	
6		6	
7		7	
8		8	
9		9	
10		10	
11		11	

6 June
Saturday
2020

PRIORITY TASKS

_____
_____
_____
_____
_____
_____

TO DO

_____
_____
_____
_____
_____
_____

NOTES

	MORNING		AFTERNOON/EVENING
12 AM		12 PM	
1		1	
2		2	
3		3	
4		4	
5		5	
6		6	
7		7	
8		8	
9		9	
10		10	
11		11	

_____
_____
_____
_____

7

June
Sunday

2020

PRIORITY TASKS

	MORNING		AFTERNOON/EVENING
12 AM		12 PM	
1		1	
2		2	
3		3	
4		4	
5		5	
6		6	
7		7	
8		8	
9		9	
10		10	
11		11	

TO DO

NOTES

8

June
Monday

2020

PRIORITY TASKS

       AFTERNOON/EVENING

	MORNING		AFTERNOON/EVENING
12 AM		12 PM	
1		1	
2		2	
3		3	
4		4	
5		5	
6		6	
7		7	
8		8	
9		9	
10		10	
11		11	

TO DO

NOTES

9 June **Tuesday** **2020**

PRIORITY TASKS

_____

_____

_____

_____

_____

_____

_____

_____

TO DO

_____

_____

_____

_____

_____

_____

_____

NOTES

MORNING		AFTERNOON/EVENING
12 AM		12 PM
1		1
2		2
3		3
4		4
5		5
6		6
7		7
8		8
9		9
10		10
11		11

_____

_____

_____

_____

10 June
Wednesday 2020

PRIORITY TASKS

_____
_____
_____
_____
_____
_____
_____
_____

TO DO

_____
_____
_____
_____
_____
_____
_____

NOTES

MORNING

12 AM	
1	
2	
3	
4	
5	
6	
7	
8	
9	
10	
11	

AFTERNOON/EVENING

12 PM	
1	
2	
3	
4	
5	
6	
7	
8	
9	
10	
11	

_____
_____
_____
_____

11 June Thursday 2020

PRIORITY TASKS

_____
_____
_____
_____
_____
_____

TO DO

_____
_____
_____
_____
_____
_____
_____
_____

NOTES

	MORNING		AFTERNOON/EVENING
12 AM		12 PM	
1		1	
2		2	
3		3	
4		4	
5		5	
6		6	
7		7	
8		8	
9		9	
10		10	
11		11	

_____
_____
_____
_____

12
June
Friday

2020

PRIORITY TASKS

MORNING

AFTERNOON/EVENING

	MORNING		AFTERNOON/EVENING
12 AM		12 PM	
1		1	
2		2	
3		3	
4		4	
5		5	
6		6	
7		7	
8		8	
9		9	
10		10	
11		11	

TO DO

NOTES

13 June Saturday 2020

PRIORITY TASKS

_____
_____
_____
_____
_____
_____
_____

TO DO

_____
_____
_____
_____
_____
_____

NOTES

MORNING		AFTERNOON/EVENING	
12 AM		12 PM	
1		1	
2		2	
3		3	
4		4	
5		5	
6		6	
7		7	
8		8	
9		9	
10		10	
11		11	

_____
_____
_____
_____

14 June Sunday   2020

PRIORITY TASKS

_____
_____
_____
_____
_____
_____
_____

TO DO

_____
_____
_____
_____
_____

NOTES

MORNING		AFTERNOON/EVENING
12 AM		12 PM
1		1
2		2
3		3
4		4
5		5
6		6
7		7
8		8
9		9
10		10
11		11

_____
_____
_____
_____

15

June
Monday

2020

PRIORITY TASKS

_____

_____

_____

_____

_____

_____

_____

TO DO

_____

_____

_____

_____

_____

_____

_____

NOTES

MORNING		AFTERNOON/EVENING	
12 AM		12 PM	
1		1	
2		2	
3		3	
4		4	
5		5	
6		6	
7		7	
8		8	
9		9	
10		10	
11		11	

_____

_____

_____

_____

16

June
Tuesday

2020

PRIORITY TASKS

MORNING		AFTERNOON/EVENING
12 AM		12 PM
1		1
2		2
3		3
4		4
5		5
6		6
7		7
8		8
9		9
10		10
11		11

TO DO

NOTES

17 June
Wednesday 2020

	MORNING		AFTERNOON/EVENING
12 AM		12 PM	
1		1	
2		2	
3		3	
4		4	
5		5	
6		6	
7		7	
8		8	
9		9	
10		10	
11		11	

TO DO

NOTES

18 June Thursday 2020

PRIORITY TASKS

_____

_____

_____

_____

_____

_____

_____

TO DO

_____

_____

_____

_____

_____

_____

_____

_____

NOTES

	MORNING		AFTERNOON/EVENING
12 AM		12 PM	
1		1	
2		2	
3		3	
4		4	
5		5	
6		6	
7		7	
8		8	
9		9	
10		10	
11		11	

_____

_____

_____

_____

19 June Friday 2020

PRIORITY TASKS

_____
_____
_____
_____
_____
_____

TO DO

_____
_____
_____
_____
_____
_____

NOTES

MORNING		AFTERNOON/EVENING	
12 AM		12 PM	
1		1	
2		2	
3		3	
4		4	
5		5	
6		6	
7		7	
8		8	
9		9	
10		10	
11		11	

_____
_____
_____
_____

20 June Saturday 2020

PRIORITY TASKS

_____
_____
_____
_____
_____
_____
_____

TO DO

_____
_____
_____
_____
_____
_____

NOTES

MORNING		AFTERNOON/EVENING	
12 AM		12 PM	
1		1	
2		2	
3		3	
4		4	
5		5	
6		6	
7		7	
8		8	
9		9	
10		10	
11		11	

_____
_____
_____
_____

21 June Sunday 2020

PRIORITY TASKS

_____
_____
_____
_____
_____
_____
_____

TO DO

_____
_____
_____
_____
_____
_____
_____

NOTES

	MORNING		AFTERNOON/EVENING
12 AM		12 PM	
1		1	
2		2	
3		3	
4		4	
5		5	
6		6	
7		7	
8		8	
9		9	
10		10	
11		11	

_____
_____
_____
_____

22 June Monday 2020

PRIORITY TASKS

	MORNING		AFTERNOON/EVENING
12 AM		12 PM	
1		1	
2		2	
3		3	
4		4	
5		5	
6		6	
7		7	
8		8	
9		9	
10		10	
11		11	

TO DO

NOTES

23 June Tuesday 2020

PRIORITY TASKS

_____

_____

_____

_____

_____

_____

TO DO

_____

_____

_____

_____

_____

_____

NOTES

	MORNING		AFTERNOON/EVENING
12 AM		12 PM	
1		1	
2		2	
3		3	
4		4	
5		5	
6		6	
7		7	
8		8	
9		9	
10		10	
11		11	

_____

_____

_____

_____

24 June Wednesday 2020

PRIORITY TASKS

_____
_____
_____
_____
_____
_____
_____

TO DO

_____
_____
_____
_____
_____
_____
_____

NOTES

	MORNING		AFTERNOON/EVENING
12 AM		12 PM	
1		1	
2		2	
3		3	
4		4	
5		5	
6		6	
7		7	
8		8	
9		9	
10		10	
11		11	

_____
_____
_____
_____

25 June
Thursday
2020

PRIORITY TASKS

_____
_____
_____
_____
_____
_____
_____

TO DO

_____
_____
_____
_____
_____
_____

NOTES

MORNING		AFTERNOON/EVENING	
12 AM		12 PM	
1		1	
2		2	
3		3	
4		4	
5		5	
6		6	
7		7	
8		8	
9		9	
10		10	
11		11	

_____
_____
_____
_____

26 June Friday 2020

PRIORITY TASKS

_____
_____
_____
_____
_____
_____
_____

TO DO

_____
_____
_____
_____
_____
_____
_____

NOTES

	MORNING		AFTERNOON/EVENING
12 AM		12 PM	
1		1	
2		2	
3		3	
4		4	
5		5	
6		6	
7		7	
8		8	
9		9	
10		10	
11		11	

_____
_____
_____
_____

27 June / **Saturday** **2020**

PRIORITY TASKS

_____
_____
_____
_____
_____
_____
_____
_____

TO DO

_____
_____
_____
_____
_____
_____
_____

NOTES

MORNING		**AFTERNOON/EVENING**
12 AM		12 PM
1		1
2		2
3		3
4		4
5		5
6		6
7		7
8		8
9		9
10		10
11		11

_____
_____
_____
_____

28

June

Sunday

2020

PRIORITY TASKS

_____

_____

_____

_____

_____

_____

_____

TO DO

_____

_____

_____

_____

_____

_____

_____

NOTES

	MORNING		AFTERNOON/EVENING
12 AM		12 PM	
1		1	
2		2	
3		3	
4		4	
5		5	
6		6	
7		7	
8		8	
9		9	
10		10	
11		11	

_____

_____

_____

_____

29
June
Monday

2020

PRIORITY TASKS

MORNING

AFTERNOON/EVENING

12 AM		12 PM	
1		1	
2		2	
3		3	
4		4	
5		5	
6		6	
7		7	
8		8	
9		9	
10		10	
11		11	

TO DO

NOTES

30 June
Tuesday **2020**

PRIORITY TASKS

_____
_____
_____
_____
_____
_____
_____

TO DO

_____
_____
_____
_____
_____
_____
_____

NOTES

MORNING		**AFTERNOON/EVENING**	
12 AM		12 PM	
1		1	
2		2	
3		3	
4		4	
5		5	
6		6	
7		7	
8		8	
9		9	
10		10	
11		11	

_____
_____
_____
_____

1 July
Wednesday 2020

PRIORITY TASKS

	MORNING		AFTERNOON/EVENING
12 AM		12 PM	
1		1	
2		2	
3		3	
4		4	
5		5	
6		6	
7		7	
8		8	
9		9	
10		10	
11		11	

TO DO

NOTES

2

July
Thursday

2020

	MORNING		AFTERNOON/EVENING
12 AM		12 PM	
1		1	
2		2	
3		3	
4		4	
5		5	
6		6	
7		7	
8		8	
9		9	
10		10	
11		11	

TO DO

NOTES

3 July Friday 2020

PRIORITY TASKS

_____
_____
_____
_____
_____
_____
_____

TO DO

_____
_____
_____
_____
_____
_____
_____

NOTES

MORNING		AFTERNOON/EVENING	
12 AM		12 PM	
1		1	
2		2	
3		3	
4		4	
5		5	
6		6	
7		7	
8		8	
9		9	
10		10	
11		11	

_____
_____
_____
_____

4

PRIORITY TASKS

_____

_____

_____

_____

_____

_____

_____

MORNING

AFTERNOON/EVENING

12 AM		12 PM	
1		1	
2		2	
3		3	
4		4	
5		5	
6		6	
7		7	
8		8	
9		9	
10		10	
11		11	

TO DO

_____

_____

_____

_____

_____

_____

_____

_____

NOTES

_____

_____

_____

_____

5 July
Sunday
2020

PRIORITY TASKS

_____
_____
_____
_____
_____
_____
_____

TO DO

_____
_____
_____
_____
_____
_____
_____
_____

NOTES

MORNING		AFTERNOON/EVENING	
12 AM		12 PM	
1		1	
2		2	
3		3	
4		4	
5		5	
6		6	
7		7	
8		8	
9		9	
10		10	
11		11	

_____
_____
_____
_____

6 July
Monday
2020

MORNING

AFTERNOON/EVENING

	MORNING			AFTERNOON/EVENING
12 AM		12 PM		
1		1		
2		2		
3		3		
4		4		
5		5		
6		6		
7		7		
8		8		
9		9		
10		10		
11		11		

TO DO

NOTES

7

July
Tuesday

2020

PRIORITY TASKS

_____

_____

_____

_____

_____

_____

TO DO

_____

_____

_____

_____

_____

_____

NOTES

	MORNING		AFTERNOON/EVENING
12 AM		12 PM	
1		1	
2		2	
3		3	
4		4	
5		5	
6		6	
7		7	
8		8	
9		9	
10		10	
11		11	

_____

_____

_____

_____

8

July
Wednesday **2020**

PRIORITY TASKS

MORNING

AFTERNOON/EVENING

12 AM		12 PM	
1		1	
2		2	
3		3	
4		4	
5		5	
6		6	
7		7	
8		8	
9		9	
10		10	
11		11	

TO DO

NOTES

9

July
Thursday

2020

PRIORITY TASKS

	MORNING		AFTERNOON/EVENING
12 AM		12 PM	
1		1	
2		2	
3		3	
4		4	
5		5	
6		6	
7		7	
8		8	
9		9	
10		10	
11		11	

TO DO

NOTES

10 July Friday 2020

	MORNING		AFTERNOON/EVENING
12 AM		12 PM	
1		1	
2		2	
3		3	
4		4	
5		5	
6		6	
7		7	
8		8	
9		9	
10		10	
11		11	

TO DO

NOTES

11 July Saturday 2020

PRIORITY TASKS

_____
_____
_____
_____
_____
_____
_____

TO DO

_____
_____
_____
_____
_____
_____
_____

NOTES

MORNING		AFTERNOON/EVENING
12 AM	12 PM	
1	1	
2	2	
3	3	
4	4	
5	5	
6	6	
7	7	
8	8	
9	9	
10	10	
11	11	

_____
_____
_____
_____

12

July
Sunday

2020

PRIORITY TASKS

_____

_____

_____

_____

_____

_____

_____

TO DO

_____

_____

_____

_____

_____

_____

_____

NOTES

_____

_____

_____

_____

MORNING		AFTERNOON/EVENING	
12 AM		12 PM	
1		1	
2		2	
3		3	
4		4	
5		5	
6		6	
7		7	
8		8	
9		9	
10		10	
11		11	

13 July Monday 2020

PRIORITY TASKS

_____
_____
_____
_____
_____
_____
_____

TO DO

_____
_____
_____
_____
_____
_____
_____

NOTES

	MORNING		AFTERNOON/EVENING
12 AM		12 PM	
1		1	
2		2	
3		3	
4		4	
5		5	
6		6	
7		7	
8		8	
9		9	
10		10	
11		11	

_____
_____
_____
_____

14 July Tuesday 2020

PRIORITY TASKS

_____

_____

_____

_____

_____

_____

TO DO

_____

_____

_____

_____

_____

_____

NOTES

MORNING		AFTERNOON/EVENING	
12 AM		12 PM	
1		1	
2		2	
3		3	
4		4	
5		5	
6		6	
7		7	
8		8	
9		9	
10		10	
11		11	

_____

_____

_____

_____

15 July
Wednesday 2020

PRIORITY TASKS

MORNING

AFTERNOON/EVENING

12 AM		12 PM
1		1
2		2
3		3
4		4
5		5
6		6
7		7
8		8
9		9
10		10
11		11

TO DO

NOTES

16

July

Thursday

2020

PRIORITY TASKS

MORNING

AFTERNOON/EVENING

12 AM		12 PM	
1		1	
2		2	
3		3	
4		4	
5		5	
6		6	
7		7	
8		8	
9		9	
10		10	
11		11	

TO DO

NOTES

17 July Friday   2020

PRIORITY TASKS

_____
_____
_____
_____
_____
_____

TO DO

_____
_____
_____
_____
_____
_____
_____

NOTES

	MORNING		AFTERNOON/EVENING
12 AM		12 PM	
1		1	
2		2	
3		3	
4		4	
5		5	
6		6	
7		7	
8		8	
9		9	
10		10	
11		11	

_____
_____
_____
_____

18 July Saturday   2020

PRIORITY TASKS

_____
_____
_____
_____
_____
_____

TO DO

_____
_____
_____
_____
_____
_____
_____

NOTES

MORNING		AFTERNOON/EVENING
12 AM	12 PM	
1	1	
2	2	
3	3	
4	4	
5	5	
6	6	
7	7	
8	8	
9	9	
10	10	
11	11	

_____
_____
_____
_____

19 July Sunday | 2020

PRIORITY TASKS

_____
_____
_____
_____
_____
_____
_____

TO DO

_____
_____
_____
_____
_____
_____
_____
_____

NOTES

MORNING		AFTERNOON/EVENING	
12 AM		12 PM	
1		1	
2		2	
3		3	
4		4	
5		5	
6		6	
7		7	
8		8	
9		9	
10		10	
11		11	

_____
_____
_____

20 July Monday 2020

PRIORITY TASKS

_____

_____

_____

_____

_____

_____

TO DO

_____

_____

_____

_____

_____

_____

NOTES

MORNING		AFTERNOON/EVENING	
12 AM		12 PM	
1		1	
2		2	
3		3	
4		4	
5		5	
6		6	
7		7	
8		8	
9		9	
10		10	
11		11	

_____

_____

_____

_____

21 July Tuesday 2020

PRIORITY TASKS

_____
_____
_____
_____
_____
_____
_____
_____

TO DO

_____
_____
_____
_____
_____
_____
_____

NOTES

	MORNING		AFTERNOON/EVENING
12 AM		12 PM	
1		1	
2		2	
3		3	
4		4	
5		5	
6		6	
7		7	
8		8	
9		9	
10		10	
11		11	

_____
_____
_____
_____

22 July
Wednesday 2020

PRIORITY TASKS

MORNING

AFTERNOON/EVENING

12 AM		12 PM	
1		1	
2		2	
3		3	
4		4	
5		5	
6		6	
7		7	
8		8	
9		9	
10		10	
11		11	

TO DO

NOTES

23 July Thursday 2020

PRIORITY TASKS

_____
_____
_____
_____
_____
_____
_____

TO DO

_____
_____
_____
_____
_____
_____
_____
_____

NOTES

MORNING		AFTERNOON/EVENING	
12 AM		12 PM	
1		1	
2		2	
3		3	
4		4	
5		5	
6		6	
7		7	
8		8	
9		9	
10		10	
11		11	

_____
_____
_____
_____

24 July Friday   2020

PRIORITY TASKS

_____
_____
_____
_____
_____
_____

TO DO

_____
_____
_____
_____
_____
_____
_____

NOTES

	MORNING		AFTERNOON/EVENING
12 AM		12 PM	
1		1	
2		2	
3		3	
4		4	
5		5	
6		6	
7		7	
8		8	
9		9	
10		10	
11		11	

_____
_____
_____
_____

25 July
Saturday
2020

PRIORITY TASKS

	MORNING		AFTERNOON/EVENING
12 AM		12 PM	
1		1	
2		2	
3		3	
4		4	
5		5	
6		6	
7		7	
8		8	
9		9	
10		10	
11		11	

TO DO

NOTES

26 July **Sunday** **2020**

	MORNING		AFTERNOON/EVENING
12 AM		12 PM	
1		1	
2		2	
3		3	
4		4	
5		5	
6		6	
7		7	
8		8	
9		9	
10		10	
11		11	

TO DO

NOTES

27 July
Monday
2020

PRIORITY TASKS

MORNING

AFTERNOON/EVENING

12 AM		12 PM	
1		1	
2		2	
3		3	
4		4	
5		5	
6		6	
7		7	
8		8	
9		9	
10		10	
11		11	

TO DO

NOTES

28 July Tuesday 2020

PRIORITY TASKS

_____

_____

_____

_____

_____

_____

TO DO

_____

_____

_____

_____

_____

_____

NOTES

	MORNING		AFTERNOON/EVENING
12 AM		12 PM	
1		1	
2		2	
3		3	
4		4	
5		5	
6		6	
7		7	
8		8	
9		9	
10		10	
11		11	

_____

_____

_____

_____

29 July Wednesday 2020

PRIORITY TASKS

_____
_____
_____
_____
_____
_____
_____

TO DO

_____
_____
_____
_____
_____
_____
_____
_____
_____

NOTES

MORNING		AFTERNOON/EVENING	
12 AM		12 PM	
1		1	
2		2	
3		3	
4		4	
5		5	
6		6	
7		7	
8		8	
9		9	
10		10	
11		11	

_____
_____
_____
_____

30

July
Thursday

2020

PRIORITY TASKS

MORNING		AFTERNOON/EVENING
12 AM		12 PM
1		1
2		2
3		3
4		4
5		5
6		6
7		7
8		8
9		9
10		10
11		11

TO DO

NOTES

31 July Friday 2020

PRIORITY TASKS

MORNING

AFTERNOON/EVENING

	MORNING		AFTERNOON/EVENING
12 AM		12 PM	
1		1	
2		2	
3		3	
4		4	
5		5	
6		6	
7		7	
8		8	
9		9	
10		10	
11		11	

TO DO

NOTES

1 August Saturday 2020

PRIORITY TASKS

_____
_____
_____
_____
_____
_____
_____
_____

TO DO

_____
_____
_____
_____
_____
_____
_____

NOTES

MORNING		AFTERNOON/EVENING	
12 AM		12 PM	
1		1	
2		2	
3		3	
4		4	
5		5	
6		6	
7		7	
8		8	
9		9	
10		10	
11		11	

_____
_____
_____
_____

2 August
Sunday

2020

PRIORITY TASKS

MORNING		AFTERNOON/EVENING
12 AM		12 PM
1		1
2		2
3		3
4		4
5		5
6		6
7		7
8		8
9		9
10		10
11		11

TO DO

NOTES

3 August
Monday

2020

PRIORITY TASKS

	MORNING		AFTERNOON/EVENING
12 AM		12 PM	
1		1	
2		2	
3		3	
4		4	
5		5	
6		6	
7		7	
8		8	
9		9	
10		10	
11		11	

TO DO

NOTES

4

August
Tuesday

2020

PRIORITY TASKS

TO DO

NOTES

	MORNING		AFTERNOON/EVENING
12 AM		12 PM	
1		1	
2		2	
3		3	
4		4	
5		5	
6		6	
7		7	
8		8	
9		9	
10		10	
11		11	

5 August
Wednesday **2020**

	MORNING		AFTERNOON/EVENING
12 AM		12 PM	
1		1	
2		2	
3		3	
4		4	
5		5	
6		6	
7		7	
8		8	
9		9	
10		10	
11		11	

TO DO

NOTES

6

August
Thursday

2020

MORNING

AFTERNOON/EVENING

12 AM		12 PM	
1		1	
2		2	
3		3	
4		4	
5		5	
6		6	
7		7	
8		8	
9		9	
10		10	
11		11	

TO DO

NOTES

7 August
Friday

2020

PRIORITY TASKS

MORNING		AFTERNOON/EVENING

	MORNING			AFTERNOON/EVENING
12 AM			12 PM	
1			1	
2			2	
3			3	
4			4	
5			5	
6			6	
7			7	
8			8	
9			9	
10			10	
11			11	

TO DO

NOTES

8 August
Saturday
2020

	MORNING		AFTERNOON/EVENING
12 AM		12 PM	
1		1	
2		2	
3		3	
4		4	
5		5	
6		6	
7		7	
8		8	
9		9	
10		10	
11		11	

TO DO

NOTES

9

PRIORITY TASKS

_____

_____

_____

_____

_____

_____

_____

TO DO

_____

_____

_____

_____

_____

_____

_____

NOTES

	MORNING		AFTERNOON/EVENING
12 AM		12 PM	
1		1	
2		2	
3		3	
4		4	
5		5	
6		6	
7		7	
8		8	
9		9	
10		10	
11		11	

_____

_____

_____

_____

10 August **Monday** **2020**

MORNING		AFTERNOON/EVENING	
12 AM		12 PM	
1		1	
2		2	
3		3	
4		4	
5		5	
6		6	
7		7	
8		8	
9		9	
10		10	
11		11	

TO DO

NOTES

11 August Tuesday   2020

PRIORITY TASKS

_____
_____
_____
_____
_____
_____
_____

TO DO

_____
_____
_____
_____
_____
_____

NOTES

MORNING		AFTERNOON/EVENING
12 AM		12 PM
1		1
2		2
3		3
4		4
5		5
6		6
7		7
8		8
9		9
10		10
11		11

_____
_____
_____
_____

12 August Wednesday 2020

PRIORITY TASKS

_____
_____
_____
_____
_____
_____

TO DO

_____
_____
_____
_____
_____
_____

NOTES

_____
_____
_____
_____

MORNING		AFTERNOON/EVENING	
12 AM		12 PM	
1		1	
2		2	
3		3	
4		4	
5		5	
6		6	
7		7	
8		8	
9		9	
10		10	
11		11	

13 August
Thursday
2020

PRIORITY TASKS

MORNING		AFTERNOON/EVENING
12 AM		12 PM
1		1
2		2
3		3
4		4
5		5
6		6
7		7
8		8
9		9
10		10
11		11

TO DO

NOTES

14 August
Friday

2020

PRIORITY TASKS

_____
_____
_____
_____
_____
_____
_____

TO DO

_____
_____
_____
_____
_____
_____
_____

NOTES

	MORNING		AFTERNOON/EVENING
12 AM		12 PM	
1		1	
2		2	
3		3	
4		4	
5		5	
6		6	
7		7	
8		8	
9		9	
10		10	
11		11	

_____
_____
_____
_____

15 August / **Saturday** **2020**

PRIORITY TASKS

_____
_____
_____
_____
_____
_____

TO DO

_____
_____
_____
_____
_____
_____

NOTES

	MORNING		AFTERNOON/EVENING
12 AM		12 PM	
1		1	
2		2	
3		3	
4		4	
5		5	
6		6	
7		7	
8		8	
9		9	
10		10	
11		11	

_____
_____
_____
_____

16

August
Sunday

2020

PRIORITY TASKS

MORNING		AFTERNOON/EVENING	
12 AM		12 PM	
1		1	
2		2	
3		3	
4		4	
5		5	
6		6	
7		7	
8		8	
9		9	
10		10	
11		11	

TO DO

NOTES

17 August Monday 2020

PRIORITY TASKS

_____
_____
_____
_____
_____
_____
_____

TO DO

_____
_____
_____
_____
_____
_____
_____

NOTES

MORNING		AFTERNOON/EVENING
12 AM		12 PM
1		1
2		2
3		3
4		4
5		5
6		6
7		7
8		8
9		9
10		10
11		11

_____
_____
_____
_____

18 August Tuesday 2020

PRIORITY TASKS

_____

_____

_____

_____

_____

_____

_____

TO DO

_____

_____

_____

_____

_____

_____

_____

NOTES

	MORNING		AFTERNOON/EVENING
12 AM		12 PM	
1		1	
2		2	
3		3	
4		4	
5		5	
6		6	
7		7	
8		8	
9		9	
10		10	
11		11	

_____

_____

_____

_____

19 August Wednesday 2020

PRIORITY TASKS

_____
_____
_____
_____
_____
_____
_____

TO DO

_____
_____
_____
_____
_____
_____

NOTES

	MORNING		AFTERNOON/EVENING
12 AM		12 PM	
1		1	
2		2	
3		3	
4		4	
5		5	
6		6	
7		7	
8		8	
9		9	
10		10	
11		11	

_____
_____
_____
_____

20 August Thursday 2020

PRIORITY TASKS

_____
_____
_____
_____
_____
_____
_____
_____

TO DO

_____
_____
_____
_____
_____
_____
_____
_____

NOTES

MORNING		AFTERNOON/EVENING	
12 AM		12 PM	
1		1	
2		2	
3		3	
4		4	
5		5	
6		6	
7		7	
8		8	
9		9	
10		10	
11		11	

_____
_____
_____
_____

21 August Friday

2020

PRIORITY TASKS

_____
_____
_____
_____
_____
_____
_____

TO DO

_____
_____
_____
_____
_____
_____
_____

NOTES

	MORNING		**AFTERNOON/EVENING**
12 AM		12 PM	
1		1	
2		2	
3		3	
4		4	
5		5	
6		6	
7		7	
8		8	
9		9	
10		10	
11		11	

_____
_____
_____
_____

22 August
Saturday
2020

PRIORITY TASKS

_____
_____
_____
_____
_____
_____
_____

TO DO

_____
_____
_____
_____
_____
_____
_____

NOTES

MORNING		AFTERNOON/EVENING
12 AM		12 PM
1		1
2		2
3		3
4		4
5		5
6		6
7		7
8		8
9		9
10		10
11		11

_____
_____
_____
_____

23 August Sunday   2020

PRIORITY TASKS

_____

_____

_____

_____

_____

_____

_____

_____

TO DO

_____

_____

_____

_____

_____

_____

_____

NOTES

MORNING		AFTERNOON/EVENING	
12 AM		12 PM	
1		1	
2		2	
3		3	
4		4	
5		5	
6		6	
7		7	
8		8	
9		9	
10		10	
11		11	

_____

_____

_____

_____

24 August
Monday
2020

PRIORITY TASKS

_____
_____
_____
_____
_____
_____
_____

TO DO

_____
_____
_____
_____
_____
_____
_____
_____
_____

NOTES

	MORNING		AFTERNOON/EVENING
12 AM		12 PM	
1		1	
2		2	
3		3	
4		4	
5		5	
6		6	
7		7	
8		8	
9		9	
10		10	
11		11	

_____
_____
_____
_____

25 August Tuesday   **2020**

PRIORITY TASKS

_____
_____
_____
_____
_____
_____
_____

TO DO

_____
_____
_____
_____
_____
_____
_____

NOTES

MORNING		AFTERNOON/EVENING	
12 AM		12 PM	
1		1	
2		2	
3		3	
4		4	
5		5	
6		6	
7		7	
8		8	
9		9	
10		10	
11		11	

_____
_____
_____
_____

26 August Wednesday 2020

PRIORITY TASKS

_____

_____

_____

_____

_____

_____

TO DO

_____

_____

_____

_____

_____

_____

_____

NOTES

MORNING		AFTERNOON/EVENING	
12 AM		12 PM	
1		1	
2		2	
3		3	
4		4	
5		5	
6		6	
7		7	
8		8	
9		9	
10		10	
11		11	

_____

_____

_____

_____

27 August **Thursday** **2020**

MORNING **AFTERNOON/EVENING**

	MORNING		AFTERNOON/EVENING
12 AM		12 PM	
1		1	
2		2	
3		3	
4		4	
5		5	
6		6	
7		7	
8		8	
9		9	
10		10	
11		11	

TO DO

NOTES

28 August
Friday

2020

PRIORITY TASKS

_____
_____
_____
_____
_____
_____
_____

TO DO

_____
_____
_____
_____
_____
_____
_____

NOTES

MORNING		AFTERNOON/EVENING	
12 AM		12 PM	
1		1	
2		2	
3		3	
4		4	
5		5	
6		6	
7		7	
8		8	
9		9	
10		10	
11		11	

_____
_____
_____
_____

29 August Saturday 2020

PRIORITY TASKS

_____
_____
_____
_____
_____
_____

TO DO

_____
_____
_____
_____
_____
_____
_____

NOTES

MORNING		AFTERNOON/EVENING	
12 AM		12 PM	
1		1	
2		2	
3		3	
4		4	
5		5	
6		6	
7		7	
8		8	
9		9	
10		10	
11		11	

_____
_____
_____
_____

30 August **Sunday** **2020**

	MORNING		AFTERNOON/EVENING
12 AM		12 PM	
1		1	
2		2	
3		3	
4		4	
5		5	
6		6	
7		7	
8		8	
9		9	
10		10	
11		11	

TO DO

NOTES

31

PRIORITY TASKS

MORNING

AFTERNOON/EVENING

	MORNING		AFTERNOON/EVENING
12 AM		12 PM	
1		1	
2		2	
3		3	
4		4	
5		5	
6		6	
7		7	
8		8	
9		9	
10		10	
11		11	

TO DO

NOTES

1 September **Tuesday** 2020

PRIORITY TASKS

_____

_____

_____

_____

_____

_____

_____

TO DO

_____

_____

_____

_____

_____

_____

_____

NOTES

	MORNING		AFTERNOON/EVENING
12 AM		12 PM	
1		1	
2		2	
3		3	
4		4	
5		5	
6		6	
7		7	
8		8	
9		9	
10		10	
11		11	

_____

_____

_____

_____

2 September
Wednesday 2020

PRIORITY TASKS

MORNING

AFTERNOON/EVENING

	MORNING		AFTERNOON/EVENING
12 AM		12 PM	
1		1	
2		2	
3		3	
4		4	
5		5	
6		6	
7		7	
8		8	
9		9	
10		10	
11		11	

TO DO

NOTES

3

September
Thursday

2020

PRIORITY TASKS

_____

_____

_____

_____

_____

_____

TO DO

_____

_____

_____

_____

_____

_____

NOTES

	MORNING		AFTERNOON/EVENING
12 AM		12 PM	
1		1	
2		2	
3		3	
4		4	
5		5	
6		6	
7		7	
8		8	
9		9	
10		10	
11		11	

_____

_____

_____

_____

4 September
Friday

2020

PRIORITY TASKS

	MORNING		AFTERNOON/EVENING
12 AM		12 PM	
1		1	
2		2	
3		3	
4		4	
5		5	
6		6	
7		7	
8		8	
9		9	
10		10	
11		11	

TO DO

NOTES

5

September
Saturday

2020

PRIORITY TASKS

MORNING

AFTERNOON/EVENING

	MORNING		AFTERNOON/EVENING
12 AM		12 PM	
1		1	
2		2	
3		3	
4		4	
5		5	
6		6	
7		7	
8		8	
9		9	
10		10	
11		11	

TO DO

NOTES

6

September
Sunday

2020

PRIORITY TASKS

_____

_____

_____

_____

_____

_____

_____

TO DO

_____

_____

_____

_____

_____

_____

_____

NOTES

	MORNING		AFTERNOON/EVENING
12 AM		12 PM	
1		1	
2		2	
3		3	
4		4	
5		5	
6		6	
7		7	
8		8	
9		9	
10		10	
11		11	

_____

_____

_____

_____

7 September
Monday
2020

PRIORITY TASKS

TO DO

NOTES

	MORNING		AFTERNOON/EVENING
12 AM		12 PM	
1		1	
2		2	
3		3	
4		4	
5		5	
6		6	
7		7	
8		8	
9		9	
10		10	
11		11	

8 September
Tuesday **2020**

PRIORITY TASKS

_____

_____

_____

_____

_____

_____

TO DO

_____

_____

_____

_____

_____

_____

NOTES

	MORNING		AFTERNOON/EVENING
12 AM		12 PM	
1		1	
2		2	
3		3	
4		4	
5		5	
6		6	
7		7	
8		8	
9		9	
10		10	
11		11	

9 September
Wednesday **2020**

PRIORITY TASKS

_____
_____
_____
_____
_____
_____
_____

TO DO

_____
_____
_____
_____
_____
_____
_____

NOTES

MORNING		AFTERNOON/EVENING	
12 AM		12 PM	
1		1	
2		2	
3		3	
4		4	
5		5	
6		6	
7		7	
8		8	
9		9	
10		10	
11		11	

_____
_____
_____
_____

10 September Thursday 2020

PRIORITY TASKS

_____
_____
_____
_____
_____
_____
_____

TO DO

_____
_____
_____
_____
_____
_____

NOTES

MORNING		AFTERNOON/EVENING
12 AM		12 PM
1		1
2		2
3		3
4		4
5		5
6		6
7		7
8		8
9		9
10		10
11		11

_____
_____
_____
_____

11 September
Friday

2020

	MORNING		AFTERNOON/EVENING
12 AM		12 PM	
1		1	
2		2	
3		3	
4		4	
5		5	
6		6	
7		7	
8		8	
9		9	
10		10	
11		11	

TO DO

NOTES

12 September Saturday 2020

PRIORITY TASKS

_____
_____
_____
_____
_____
_____
_____

TO DO

_____
_____
_____
_____
_____
_____
_____

NOTES

MORNING		AFTERNOON/EVENING	
12 AM		12 PM	
1		1	
2		2	
3		3	
4		4	
5		5	
6		6	
7		7	
8		8	
9		9	
10		10	
11		11	

_____
_____
_____
_____

13 September Sunday 2020

PRIORITY TASKS

_____

_____

_____

_____

_____

_____

TO DO

_____

_____

_____

_____

_____

_____

NOTES

MORNING		AFTERNOON/EVENING	
12 AM		12 PM	
1		1	
2		2	
3		3	
4		4	
5		5	
6		6	
7		7	
8		8	
9		9	
10		10	
11		11	

_____

_____

_____

_____

14 September
Monday
2020

PRIORITY TASKS

TO DO

NOTES

	MORNING		AFTERNOON/EVENING
12 AM		12 PM	
1		1	
2		2	
3		3	
4		4	
5		5	
6		6	
7		7	
8		8	
9		9	
10		10	
11		11	

15 September
Tuesday

2020

PRIORITY TASKS

_____
_____
_____
_____
_____
_____
_____
_____

TO DO

_____
_____
_____
_____
_____
_____
_____

NOTES

	MORNING		**AFTERNOON/EVENING**
12 AM		12 PM	
1		1	
2		2	
3		3	
4		4	
5		5	
6		6	
7		7	
8		8	
9		9	
10		10	
11		11	

_____
_____
_____
_____

16 September Wednesday 2020

PRIORITY TASKS

_____

_____

_____

_____

_____

_____

_____

TO DO

_____

_____

_____

_____

_____

NOTES

	MORNING		AFTERNOON/EVENING
12 AM		12 PM	
1		1	
2		2	
3		3	
4		4	
5		5	
6		6	
7		7	
8		8	
9		9	
10		10	
11		11	

_____

_____

_____

_____

17

September
Thursday

2020

PRIORITY TASKS

TO DO

NOTES

	MORNING		AFTERNOON/EVENING
12 AM		12 PM	
1		1	
2		2	
3		3	
4		4	
5		5	
6		6	
7		7	
8		8	
9		9	
10		10	
11		11	

18 September
Friday
2020

PRIORITY TASKS

MORNING | AFTERNOON/EVENING

	MORNING		AFTERNOON/EVENING
12 AM		12 PM	
1		1	
2		2	
3		3	
4		4	
5		5	
6		6	
7		7	
8		8	
9		9	
10		10	
11		11	

TO DO

NOTES

19 September Saturday 2020

PRIORITY TASKS

_____

_____

_____

_____

_____

_____

_____

TO DO

_____

_____

_____

_____

_____

_____

_____

NOTES

MORNING		AFTERNOON/EVENING
12 AM	12 PM	
1	1	
2	2	
3	3	
4	4	
5	5	
6	6	
7	7	
8	8	
9	9	
10	10	
11	11	

_____

_____

_____

_____

20 September
Sunday
2020

PRIORITY TASKS

MORNING

AFTERNOON/EVENING

	MORNING		AFTERNOON/EVENING
12 AM		12 PM	
1		1	
2		2	
3		3	
4		4	
5		5	
6		6	
7		7	
8		8	
9		9	
10		10	
11		11	

TO DO

NOTES

21 September
Monday

2020

PRIORITY TASKS

MORNING

AFTERNOON/EVENING

12 AM		12 PM	
1		1	
2		2	
3		3	
4		4	
5		5	
6		6	
7		7	
8		8	
9		9	
10		10	
11		11	

TO DO

NOTES

22 September
Tuesday

2020

PRIORITY TASKS

_____

_____

_____

_____

_____

_____

_____

TO DO

_____

_____

_____

_____

_____

_____

NOTES

MORNING		AFTERNOON/EVENING	
12 AM		12 PM	
1		1	
2		2	
3		3	
4		4	
5		5	
6		6	
7		7	
8		8	
9		9	
10		10	
11		11	

_____

_____

_____

_____

23 September Wednesday 2020

PRIORITY TASKS

_____
_____
_____
_____
_____
_____
_____

TO DO

_____
_____
_____
_____
_____
_____
_____

NOTES

MORNING		AFTERNOON/EVENING	
12 AM		12 PM	
1		1	
2		2	
3		3	
4		4	
5		5	
6		6	
7		7	
8		8	
9		9	
10		10	
11		11	

_____
_____
_____
_____

24 September Thursday 2020

PRIORITY TASKS

_____
_____
_____
_____
_____
_____

TO DO

_____
_____
_____
_____
_____
_____

NOTES

	MORNING		AFTERNOON/EVENING
12 AM		12 PM	
1		1	
2		2	
3		3	
4		4	
5		5	
6		6	
7		7	
8		8	
9		9	
10		10	
11		11	

_____
_____
_____
_____

25 September Friday 2020

PRIORITY TASKS

_____
_____
_____
_____
_____
_____
_____

TO DO

_____
_____
_____
_____
_____
_____

NOTES

	MORNING		AFTERNOON/EVENING
12 AM		12 PM	
1		1	
2		2	
3		3	
4		4	
5		5	
6		6	
7		7	
8		8	
9		9	
10		10	
11		11	

_____
_____
_____
_____

26 September / Saturday 2020

PRIORITY TASKS

_____
_____
_____
_____
_____
_____
_____

TO DO

_____
_____
_____
_____
_____
_____

NOTES

_____
_____
_____
_____

	MORNING		AFTERNOON/EVENING
12 AM		12 PM	
1		1	
2		2	
3		3	
4		4	
5		5	
6		6	
7		7	
8		8	
9		9	
10		10	
11		11	

27 September Sunday 2020

PRIORITY TASKS

_____
_____
_____
_____
_____
_____
_____

TO DO

_____
_____
_____
_____
_____
_____
_____

NOTES

MORNING		AFTERNOON/EVENING	
12 AM		12 PM	
1		1	
2		2	
3		3	
4		4	
5		5	
6		6	
7		7	
8		8	
9		9	
10		10	
11		11	

28 September Monday 2020

PRIORITY TASKS

_____
_____
_____
_____
_____
_____
_____

TO DO

_____
_____
_____
_____
_____
_____
_____

NOTES

MORNING		AFTERNOON/EVENING	
12 AM		12 PM	
1		1	
2		2	
3		3	
4		4	
5		5	
6		6	
7		7	
8		8	
9		9	
10		10	
11		11	

_____
_____
_____
_____

29 September Tuesday 2020

PRIORITY TASKS

_____
_____
_____
_____
_____
_____
_____

TO DO

_____
_____
_____
_____
_____
_____

NOTES

	MORNING		AFTERNOON/EVENING
12 AM		12 PM	
1		1	
2		2	
3		3	
4		4	
5		5	
6		6	
7		7	
8		8	
9		9	
10		10	
11		11	

_____
_____
_____
_____

30 September Wednesday 2020

PRIORITY TASKS

_____
_____
_____
_____
_____
_____
_____
_____

TO DO

_____
_____
_____
_____
_____
_____
_____
_____

NOTES

MORNING		AFTERNOON/EVENING	
12 AM		12 PM	
1		1	
2		2	
3		3	
4		4	
5		5	
6		6	
7		7	
8		8	
9		9	
10		10	
11		11	

_____
_____
_____
_____

1

October
Thursday

2020

PRIORITY TASKS

MORNING

AFTERNOON/EVENING

	MORNING		AFTERNOON/EVENING
12 AM		12 PM	
1		1	
2		2	
3		3	
4		4	
5		5	
6		6	
7		7	
8		8	
9		9	
10		10	
11		11	

TO DO

NOTES

2 October
Friday
2020

PRIORITY TASKS

MORNING

AFTERNOON/EVENING

12 AM		12 PM	
1		1	
2		2	
3		3	
4		4	
5		5	
6		6	
7		7	
8		8	
9		9	
10		10	
11		11	

TO DO

NOTES

3 October
Saturday
2020

PRIORITY TASKS

_____
_____
_____
_____
_____
_____

TO DO

_____
_____
_____
_____
_____
_____

NOTES

_____
_____
_____
_____

MORNING

12 AM		12 PM	
1		1	
2		2	
3		3	
4		4	
5		5	
6		6	
7		7	
8		8	
9		9	
10		10	
11		11	

AFTERNOON/EVENING

4 October Sunday 2020

PRIORITY TASKS

_____
_____
_____
_____
_____
_____
_____
_____

TO DO

_____
_____
_____
_____
_____
_____
_____

NOTES

MORNING		AFTERNOON/EVENING	
12 AM		12 PM	
1		1	
2		2	
3		3	
4		4	
5		5	
6		6	
7		7	
8		8	
9		9	
10		10	
11		11	

_____
_____
_____
_____

5 October
Monday

2020

PRIORITY TASKS

TO DO

NOTES

	MORNING		AFTERNOON/EVENING
12 AM		12 PM	
1		1	
2		2	
3		3	
4		4	
5		5	
6		6	
7		7	
8		8	
9		9	
10		10	
11		11	

6 October
Tuesday

2020

PRIORITY TASKS

	MORNING		AFTERNOON/EVENING
12 AM		12 PM	
1		1	
2		2	
3		3	
4		4	
5		5	
6		6	
7		7	
8		8	
9		9	
10		10	
11		11	

TO DO

NOTES

7 October **Wednesday** 2020

PRIORITY TASKS

_____

_____

_____

_____

_____

_____

_____

TO DO

_____

_____

_____

_____

_____

_____

_____

_____

NOTES

MORNING		**AFTERNOON/EVENING**	
12 AM		12 PM	
1		1	
2		2	
3		3	
4		4	
5		5	
6		6	
7		7	
8		8	
9		9	
10		10	
11		11	

_____

_____

_____

_____

8 October
Thursday **2020**

	MORNING		AFTERNOON/EVENING
12 AM		12 PM	
1		1	
2		2	
3		3	
4		4	
5		5	
6		6	
7		7	
8		8	
9		9	
10		10	
11		11	

TO DO

NOTES

9

October
Friday

2020

PRIORITY TASKS

	MORNING		AFTERNOON/EVENING
12 AM		12 PM	
1		1	
2		2	
3		3	
4		4	
5		5	
6		6	
7		7	
8		8	
9		9	
10		10	
11		11	

TO DO

NOTES

10 October Saturday 2020

PRIORITY TASKS

_____
_____
_____
_____
_____
_____
_____

TO DO

_____
_____
_____
_____
_____
_____
_____

NOTES

MORNING		AFTERNOON/EVENING
12 AM		12 PM
1		1
2		2
3		3
4		4
5		5
6		6
7		7
8		8
9		9
10		10
11		11

_____
_____
_____
_____

11 October
Sunday
2020

PRIORITY TASKS

	MORNING		AFTERNOON/EVENING
12 AM		12 PM	
1		1	
2		2	
3		3	
4		4	
5		5	
6		6	
7		7	
8		8	
9		9	
10		10	
11		11	

TO DO

NOTES

12 October
Monday

2020

PRIORITY TASKS

MORNING

AFTERNOON/EVENING

	MORNING		AFTERNOON/EVENING
12 AM		12 PM	
1		1	
2		2	
3		3	
4		4	
5		5	
6		6	
7		7	
8		8	
9		9	
10		10	
11		11	

TO DO

NOTES

13

October
Tuesday

2020

PRIORITY TASKS

MORNING		AFTERNOON/EVENING	
12 AM		12 PM	
1		1	
2		2	
3		3	
4		4	
5		5	
6		6	
7		7	
8		8	
9		9	
10		10	
11		11	

TO DO

NOTES

14 October
Wednesday 2020

PRIORITY TASKS

_____

_____

_____

_____

_____

_____

_____

TO DO

_____

_____

_____

_____

_____

_____

_____

_____

NOTES

MORNING		AFTERNOON/EVENING	
12 AM		12 PM	
1		1	
2		2	
3		3	
4		4	
5		5	
6		6	
7		7	
8		8	
9		9	
10		10	
11		11	

_____

_____

_____

_____

15 October
Thursday
2020

PRIORITY TASKS

MORNING			AFTERNOON/EVENING
12 AM		12 PM	
1		1	
2		2	
3		3	
4		4	
5		5	
6		6	
7		7	
8		8	
9		9	
10		10	
11		11	

TO DO

NOTES

16 October
Friday

2020

MORNING			AFTERNOON/EVENING
12 AM		12 PM	
1		1	
2		2	
3		3	
4		4	
5		5	
6		6	
7		7	
8		8	
9		9	
10		10	
11		11	

TO DO

NOTES

17 October **Saturday** **2020**

PRIORITY TASKS

MORNING | AFTERNOON/EVENING

12 AM		12 PM	
1		1	
2		2	
3		3	
4		4	
5		5	
6		6	
7		7	
8		8	
9		9	
10		10	
11		11	

TO DO

NOTES

18 October
Sunday

2020

PRIORITY TASKS

_____

_____

_____

_____

_____

_____

_____

TO DO

_____

_____

_____

_____

_____

_____

_____

_____

_____

NOTES

	MORNING		AFTERNOON/EVENING
12 AM		12 PM	
1		1	
2		2	
3		3	
4		4	
5		5	
6		6	
7		7	
8		8	
9		9	
10		10	
11		11	

_____

_____

_____

_____

19

October
Monday

2020

MORNING

AFTERNOON/EVENING

	MORNING		AFTERNOON/EVENING
12 AM		12 PM	
1		1	
2		2	
3		3	
4		4	
5		5	
6		6	
7		7	
8		8	
9		9	
10		10	
11		11	

TO DO

NOTES

20 October
Tuesday

2020

PRIORITY TASKS

_____
_____
_____
_____
_____
_____
_____
_____

TO DO

_____
_____
_____
_____
_____
_____
_____

NOTES

	MORNING		AFTERNOON/EVENING
12 AM		12 PM	
1		1	
2		2	
3		3	
4		4	
5		5	
6		6	
7		7	
8		8	
9		9	
10		10	
11		11	

_____
_____
_____
_____

21 October
Wednesday 2020

PRIORITY TASKS

MORNING

AFTERNOON/EVENING

12 AM		12 PM	
1		1	
2		2	
3		3	
4		4	
5		5	
6		6	
7		7	
8		8	
9		9	
10		10	
11		11	

TO DO

NOTES

22 October **Thursday** 2020

PRIORITY TASKS

_____
_____
_____
_____
_____
_____
_____

TO DO

_____
_____
_____
_____
_____
_____
_____

NOTES

MORNING		AFTERNOON/EVENING	
12 AM		12 PM	
1		1	
2		2	
3		3	
4		4	
5		5	
6		6	
7		7	
8		8	
9		9	
10		10	
11		11	

_____
_____
_____
_____

23 October Friday 2020

PRIORITY TASKS

MORNING

AFTERNOON/EVENING

	MORNING		AFTERNOON/EVENING
12 AM		12 PM	
1		1	
2		2	
3		3	
4		4	
5		5	
6		6	
7		7	
8		8	
9		9	
10		10	
11		11	

TO DO

NOTES

24 October Saturday 2020

PRIORITY TASKS

_____
_____
_____
_____
_____
_____

TO DO

_____
_____
_____
_____
_____
_____
_____

NOTES

MORNING		AFTERNOON/EVENING	
12 AM		12 PM	
1		1	
2		2	
3		3	
4		4	
5		5	
6		6	
7		7	
8		8	
9		9	
10		10	
11		11	

_____
_____
_____
_____

25 October
Sunday

2020

PRIORITY TASKS

_____
_____
_____
_____
_____
_____

TO DO

_____
_____
_____
_____
_____
_____
_____

NOTES

	MORNING		AFTERNOON/EVENING
12 AM		12 PM	
1		1	
2		2	
3		3	
4		4	
5		5	
6		6	
7		7	
8		8	
9		9	
10		10	
11		11	

_____
_____
_____
_____

26 October Monday 2020

PRIORITY TASKS

_____
_____
_____
_____
_____
_____
_____

TO DO

_____
_____
_____
_____
_____
_____
_____

NOTES

	MORNING		AFTERNOON/EVENING
12 AM		12 PM	
1		1	
2		2	
3		3	
4		4	
5		5	
6		6	
7		7	
8		8	
9		9	
10		10	
11		11	

_____
_____
_____
_____

27 October
Tuesday

2020

PRIORITY TASKS

_____
_____
_____
_____
_____
_____
_____

TO DO

_____
_____
_____
_____
_____
_____

NOTES

MORNING		**AFTERNOON/EVENING**	
12 AM		12 PM	
1		1	
2		2	
3		3	
4		4	
5		5	
6		6	
7		7	
8		8	
9		9	
10		10	
11		11	

_____
_____
_____
_____

28 October Wednesday 2020

PRIORITY TASKS

_____
_____
_____
_____
_____
_____
_____

TO DO

_____
_____
_____
_____
_____
_____

NOTES

	MORNING		AFTERNOON/EVENING
12 AM		12 PM	
1		1	
2		2	
3		3	
4		4	
5		5	
6		6	
7		7	
8		8	
9		9	
10		10	
11		11	

_____
_____
_____
_____

29 October
Thursday **2020**

PRIORITY TASKS

_____

_____

_____

_____

_____

_____

TO DO

_____

_____

_____

_____

_____

_____

NOTES

MORNING		AFTERNOON/EVENING	
12 AM		12 PM	
1		1	
2		2	
3		3	
4		4	
5		5	
6		6	
7		7	
8		8	
9		9	
10		10	
11		11	

_____

_____

_____

_____

30 October
Friday

2020

PRIORITY TASKS

MORNING

AFTERNOON/EVENING

12 AM		12 PM	
1		1	
2		2	
3		3	
4		4	
5		5	
6		6	
7		7	
8		8	
9		9	
10		10	
11		11	

TO DO

NOTES

31 October Saturday 2020

PRIORITY TASKS

_____
_____
_____
_____
_____
_____
_____

TO DO

_____
_____
_____
_____
_____
_____

NOTES

	MORNING		AFTERNOON/EVENING
12 AM		12 PM	
1		1	
2		2	
3		3	
4		4	
5		5	
6		6	
7		7	
8		8	
9		9	
10		10	
11		11	

_____
_____
_____
_____

1

November
Sunday

2020

PRIORITY TASKS

MORNING

AFTERNOON/EVENING

	MORNING		AFTERNOON/EVENING
12 AM		12 PM	
1		1	
2		2	
3		3	
4		4	
5		5	
6		6	
7		7	
8		8	
9		9	
10		10	
11		11	

TO DO

NOTES

2 November
Monday
2020

	MORNING		AFTERNOON/EVENING
12 AM		12 PM	
1		1	
2		2	
3		3	
4		4	
5		5	
6		6	
7		7	
8		8	
9		9	
10		10	
11		11	

TO DO

NOTES

3 November
Tuesday
2020

PRIORITY TASKS

_____

_____

_____

_____

_____

_____

_____

TO DO

_____

_____

_____

_____

_____

_____

_____

NOTES

	MORNING		AFTERNOON/EVENING
12 AM		12 PM	
1		1	
2		2	
3		3	
4		4	
5		5	
6		6	
7		7	
8		8	
9		9	
10		10	
11		11	

_____

_____

_____

_____

4

November
Wednesday 2020

PRIORITY TASKS

MORNING

AFTERNOON/EVENING

	MORNING		AFTERNOON/EVENING
12 AM		12 PM	
1		1	
2		2	
3		3	
4		4	
5		5	
6		6	
7		7	
8		8	
9		9	
10		10	
11		11	

TO DO

NOTES

5

November
Thursday

2020

PRIORITY TASKS

_____

_____

_____

_____

_____

_____

_____

TO DO

_____

_____

_____

_____

_____

_____

_____

NOTES

	MORNING		AFTERNOON/EVENING
12 AM		12 PM	
1		1	
2		2	
3		3	
4		4	
5		5	
6		6	
7		7	
8		8	
9		9	
10		10	
11		11	

_____

_____

_____

_____

6 November
Friday

2020

PRIORITY TASKS

MORNING

AFTERNOON/EVENING

12 AM		12 PM	
1		1	
2		2	
3		3	
4		4	
5		5	
6		6	
7		7	
8		8	
9		9	
10		10	
11		11	

TO DO

NOTES

7

November
Saturday

2020

PRIORITY TASKS

MORNING

AFTERNOON/EVENING

	MORNING		AFTERNOON/EVENING
12 AM		12 PM	
1		1	
2		2	
3		3	
4		4	
5		5	
6		6	
7		7	
8		8	
9		9	
10		10	
11		11	

TO DO

NOTES

8

November
Sunday

2020

PRIORITY TASKS

MORNING			AFTERNOON/EVENING
12 AM		12 PM	
1		1	
2		2	
3		3	
4		4	
5		5	
6		6	
7		7	
8		8	
9		9	
10		10	
11		11	

TO DO

NOTES

9 November
Monday
2020

PRIORITY TASKS

MORNING

AFTERNOON/EVENING

	MORNING			AFTERNOON/EVENING
12 AM		12 PM		
1		1		
2		2		
3		3		
4		4		
5		5		
6		6		
7		7		
8		8		
9		9		
10		10		
11		11		

TO DO

NOTES

10 November
Tuesday

2020

PRIORITY TASKS

	MORNING		AFTERNOON/EVENING
12 AM		12 PM	
1		1	
2		2	
3		3	
4		4	
5		5	
6		6	
7		7	
8		8	
9		9	
10		10	
11		11	

TO DO

NOTES

11 November Wednesday 2020

	MORNING		AFTERNOON/EVENING
12 AM		12 PM	
1		1	
2		2	
3		3	
4		4	
5		5	
6		6	
7		7	
8		8	
9		9	
10		10	
11		11	

TO DO

NOTES

12 November **Thursday** 2020

PRIORITY TASKS

_____

_____

_____

_____

_____

_____

TO DO

_____

_____

_____

_____

_____

NOTES

MORNING		AFTERNOON/EVENING	
12 AM		12 PM	
1		1	
2		2	
3		3	
4		4	
5		5	
6		6	
7		7	
8		8	
9		9	
10		10	
11		11	

_____

_____

_____

_____

13 November Friday 2020

PRIORITY TASKS

_____
_____
_____
_____
_____
_____
_____

TO DO

_____
_____
_____
_____
_____
_____

NOTES

MORNING		AFTERNOON/EVENING
12 AM		12 PM
1		1
2		2
3		3
4		4
5		5
6		6
7		7
8		8
9		9
10		10
11		11

_____
_____
_____
_____

14 November Saturday   2020

PRIORITY TASKS

_____

_____

_____

_____

_____

_____

_____

TO DO

_____

_____

_____

_____

_____

_____

NOTES

	MORNING		AFTERNOON/EVENING
12 AM		12 PM	
1		1	
2		2	
3		3	
4		4	
5		5	
6		6	
7		7	
8		8	
9		9	
10		10	
11		11	

_____

_____

_____

_____

15

November
Sunday

2020

PRIORITY TASKS

_____

_____

_____

_____

_____

_____

_____

TO DO

_____

_____

_____

_____

_____

_____

_____

NOTES

MORNING		AFTERNOON/EVENING	
12 AM		12 PM	
1		1	
2		2	
3		3	
4		4	
5		5	
6		6	
7		7	
8		8	
9		9	
10		10	
11		11	

_____

_____

_____

_____

16 November
Monday

2020

PRIORITY TASKS

MORNING		AFTERNOON/EVENING	
12 AM		12 PM	
1		1	
2		2	
3		3	
4		4	
5		5	
6		6	
7		7	
8		8	
9		9	
10		10	
11		11	

TO DO

NOTES

17 November
Tuesday
2020

PRIORITY TASKS

MORNING		AFTERNOON/EVENING	
12 AM		12 PM	
1		1	
2		2	
3		3	
4		4	
5		5	
6		6	
7		7	
8		8	
9		9	
10		10	
11		11	

TO DO

NOTES

18 November
Wednesday **2020**

PRIORITY TASKS

_____

_____

_____

_____

_____

_____

TO DO

_____

_____

_____

_____

_____

_____

NOTES

MORNING		**AFTERNOON/EVENING**
12 AM		12 PM
1		1
2		2
3		3
4		4
5		5
6		6
7		7
8		8
9		9
10		10
11		11

_____

_____

_____

_____

19 November **Thursday** 2020

PRIORITY TASKS

_____

_____

_____

_____

_____

_____

TO DO

_____

_____

_____

_____

_____

_____

NOTES

MORNING		AFTERNOON/EVENING	
12 AM		12 PM	
1		1	
2		2	
3		3	
4		4	
5		5	
6		6	
7		7	
8		8	
9		9	
10		10	
11		11	

_____

_____

_____

_____

20 November Friday 2020

PRIORITY TASKS

_____
_____
_____
_____
_____
_____
_____

TO DO

_____
_____
_____
_____
_____
_____
_____

NOTES

MORNING		AFTERNOON/EVENING	
12 AM		12 PM	
1		1	
2		2	
3		3	
4		4	
5		5	
6		6	
7		7	
8		8	
9		9	
10		10	
11		11	

_____
_____
_____
_____

21

November
Saturday

2020

	MORNING		AFTERNOON/EVENING
12 AM		12 PM	
1		1	
2		2	
3		3	
4		4	
5		5	
6		6	
7		7	
8		8	
9		9	
10		10	
11		11	

TO DO

NOTES

PRIORITY TASKS

MORNING   AFTERNOON/EVENING

12 AM		12 PM	
1		1	
2		2	
3		3	
4		4	
5		5	
6		6	
7		7	
8		8	
9		9	
10		10	
11		11	

TO DO

NOTES

23 November Monday 2020

PRIORITY TASKS

_____
_____
_____
_____
_____
_____
_____

TO DO

_____
_____
_____
_____
_____
_____
_____

NOTES

	MORNING		AFTERNOON/EVENING
12 AM		12 PM	
1		1	
2		2	
3		3	
4		4	
5		5	
6		6	
7		7	
8		8	
9		9	
10		10	
11		11	

_____
_____
_____
_____

24 November
Tuesday

2020

PRIORITY TASKS

_____

_____

_____

_____

_____

_____

_____

TO DO

_____

_____

_____

_____

_____

_____

_____

NOTES

	MORNING		**AFTERNOON/EVENING**
12 AM		12 PM	
1		1	
2		2	
3		3	
4		4	
5		5	
6		6	
7		7	
8		8	
9		9	
10		10	
11		11	

_____

_____

_____

_____

25 November Wednesday 2020

PRIORITY TASKS

_____
_____
_____
_____
_____
_____
_____

TO DO

_____
_____
_____
_____
_____
_____
_____

NOTES

MORNING		AFTERNOON/EVENING	
12 AM		12 PM	
1		1	
2		2	
3		3	
4		4	
5		5	
6		6	
7		7	
8		8	
9		9	
10		10	
11		11	

_____
_____
_____
_____

26 November Thursday 2020

PRIORITY TASKS

_____
_____
_____
_____
_____
_____
_____

TO DO

_____
_____
_____
_____
_____
_____
_____

NOTES

	MORNING		AFTERNOON/EVENING
12 AM		12 PM	
1		1	
2		2	
3		3	
4		4	
5		5	
6		6	
7		7	
8		8	
9		9	
10		10	
11		11	

_____
_____
_____
_____

27 November Friday   2020

PRIORITY TASKS

_____

_____

_____

_____

_____

_____

_____

TO DO

_____

_____

_____

_____

_____

_____

_____

NOTES

MORNING

	AFTERNOON/EVENING
12 AM	12 PM
1	1
2	2
3	3
4	4
5	5
6	6
7	7
8	8
9	9
10	10
11	11

_____

_____

_____

_____

28 November / **Saturday** / **2020**

PRIORITY TASKS

_____
_____
_____
_____
_____
_____

TO DO

_____
_____
_____
_____
_____
_____

NOTES

MORNING		AFTERNOON/EVENING	
12 AM		12 PM	
1		1	
2		2	
3		3	
4		4	
5		5	
6		6	
7		7	
8		8	
9		9	
10		10	
11		11	

_____
_____
_____
_____

29 November
Sunday
2020

MORNING		AFTERNOON/EVENING
12 AM		12 PM
1		1
2		2
3		3
4		4
5		5
6		6
7		7
8		8
9		9
10		10
11		11

TO DO

NOTES

30 November
Monday
2020

PRIORITY TASKS

_____
_____
_____
_____
_____
_____

TO DO

_____
_____
_____
_____
_____
_____
_____

NOTES

_____
_____
_____
_____

MORNING		**AFTERNOON/EVENING**	
12 AM		12 PM	
1		1	
2		2	
3		3	
4		4	
5		5	
6		6	
7		7	
8		8	
9		9	
10		10	
11		11	

1

December
Tuesday

2020

PRIORITY TASKS

MORNING

AFTERNOON/EVENING

	12 AM		12 PM	
	1		1	
	2		2	
	3		3	
	4		4	
	5		5	
	6		6	
	7		7	
	8		8	
	9		9	
	10		10	
	11		11	

TO DO

NOTES

2 December **Wednesday** 2020

PRIORITY TASKS

_____

_____

_____

_____

_____

_____

TO DO

_____

_____

_____

_____

_____

_____

NOTES

MORNING		AFTERNOON/EVENING	
12 AM		12 PM	
1		1	
2		2	
3		3	
4		4	
5		5	
6		6	
7		7	
8		8	
9		9	
10		10	
11		11	

_____

_____

_____

_____

3 December
Thursday **2020**

PRIORITY TASKS

_____
_____
_____
_____
_____
_____

TO DO

_____
_____
_____
_____
_____
_____

NOTES

MORNING		AFTERNOON/EVENING	
12 AM		12 PM	
1		1	
2		2	
3		3	
4		4	
5		5	
6		6	
7		7	
8		8	
9		9	
10		10	
11		11	

_____
_____
_____
_____

4 December
Friday
2020

	MORNING		AFTERNOON/EVENING
12 AM		12 PM	
1		1	
2		2	
3		3	
4		4	
5		5	
6		6	
7		7	
8		8	
9		9	
10		10	
11		11	

TO DO

NOTES

5 December
Saturday
2020

PRIORITY TASKS

_____
_____
_____
_____
_____
_____
_____

TO DO

_____
_____
_____
_____
_____
_____

NOTES

	MORNING		AFTERNOON/EVENING
12 AM		12 PM	
1		1	
2		2	
3		3	
4		4	
5		5	
6		6	
7		7	
8		8	
9		9	
10		10	
11		11	

_____
_____
_____
_____

6 December
Sunday
2020

PRIORITY TASKS

MORNING

AFTERNOON/EVENING

12 AM		12 PM	
1		1	
2		2	
3		3	
4		4	
5		5	
6		6	
7		7	
8		8	
9		9	
10		10	
11		11	

TO DO

NOTES

7 December
Monday **2020**

	MORNING		AFTERNOON/EVENING
12 AM		12 PM	
1		1	
2		2	
3		3	
4		4	
5		5	
6		6	
7		7	
8		8	
9		9	
10		10	
11		11	

TO DO

NOTES

8

December
Tuesday

2020

PRIORITY TASKS

MORNING

AFTERNOON/EVENING

12 AM		12 PM	
1		1	
2		2	
3		3	
4		4	
5		5	
6		6	
7		7	
8		8	
9		9	
10		10	
11		11	

TO DO

NOTES

9

December
Wednesday **2020**

PRIORITY TASKS

MORNING

AFTERNOON/EVENING

	MORNING		AFTERNOON/EVENING
12 AM		12 PM	
1		1	
2		2	
3		3	
4		4	
5		5	
6		6	
7		7	
8		8	
9		9	
10		10	
11		11	

TO DO

NOTES

10 December Thursday 2020

PRIORITY TASKS

_____
_____
_____
_____
_____
_____
_____

TO DO

_____
_____
_____
_____
_____
_____
_____

NOTES

	MORNING		AFTERNOON/EVENING
12 AM		12 PM	
1		1	
2		2	
3		3	
4		4	
5		5	
6		6	
7		7	
8		8	
9		9	
10		10	
11		11	

_____
_____
_____
_____

11 December
Friday

2020

PRIORITY TASKS

_____
_____
_____
_____
_____
_____
_____

TO DO

_____
_____
_____
_____
_____
_____
_____

NOTES

	MORNING		AFTERNOON/EVENING
12 AM		12 PM	
1		1	
2		2	
3		3	
4		4	
5		5	
6		6	
7		7	
8		8	
9		9	
10		10	
11		11	

_____
_____
_____
_____

12 December
Saturday
2020

PRIORITY TASKS

	MORNING		AFTERNOON/EVENING
12 AM		12 PM	
1		1	
2		2	
3		3	
4		4	
5		5	
6		6	
7		7	
8		8	
9		9	
10		10	
11		11	

TO DO

NOTES

13 December Sunday 2020

PRIORITY TASKS

_____

_____

_____

_____

_____

_____

TO DO

_____

_____

_____

_____

_____

_____

NOTES

MORNING		AFTERNOON/EVENING	
12 AM		12 PM	
1		1	
2		2	
3		3	
4		4	
5		5	
6		6	
7		7	
8		8	
9		9	
10		10	
11		11	

_____

_____

_____

_____

14 December
Monday

2020

PRIORITY TASKS

_____
_____
_____
_____
_____
_____
_____

TO DO

_____
_____
_____
_____
_____
_____

NOTES

	MORNING			AFTERNOON/EVENING
12 AM			12 PM	
1			1	
2			2	
3			3	
4			4	
5			5	
6			6	
7			7	
8			8	
9			9	
10			10	
11			11	

_____
_____
_____
_____

15 December
Tuesday **2020**

_____

_____

_____

_____

_____

_____

_____

TO DO

_____

_____

_____

_____

_____

_____

NOTES

	MORNING		AFTERNOON/EVENING
12 AM		12 PM	
1		1	
2		2	
3		3	
4		4	
5		5	
6		6	
7		7	
8		8	
9		9	
10		10	
11		11	

_____

_____

_____

_____

16 December
Wednesday 2020

PRIORITY TASKS

_____
_____
_____
_____
_____
_____
_____

TO DO

_____
_____
_____
_____
_____
_____
_____

NOTES

	MORNING		AFTERNOON/EVENING
12 AM		12 PM	
1		1	
2		2	
3		3	
4		4	
5		5	
6		6	
7		7	
8		8	
9		9	
10		10	
11		11	

_____
_____
_____
_____

17 December Thursday 2020

PRIORITY TASKS

_____
_____
_____
_____
_____
_____
_____
_____

TO DO

_____
_____
_____
_____
_____
_____
_____

NOTES

MORNING		AFTERNOON/EVENING	
12 AM		12 PM	
1		1	
2		2	
3		3	
4		4	
5		5	
6		6	
7		7	
8		8	
9		9	
10		10	
11		11	

_____
_____
_____
_____

18 December Friday 2020

MORNING		AFTERNOON/EVENING	
12 AM		12 PM	
1		1	
2		2	
3		3	
4		4	
5		5	
6		6	
7		7	
8		8	
9		9	
10		10	
11		11	

TO DO

NOTES

19 December **Saturday** **2020**

PRIORITY TASKS

_____
_____
_____
_____
_____
_____
_____

TO DO

_____
_____
_____
_____
_____
_____
_____

NOTES

_____
_____
_____
_____

MORNING		AFTERNOON/EVENING	
12 AM		12 PM	
1		1	
2		2	
3		3	
4		4	
5		5	
6		6	
7		7	
8		8	
9		9	
10		10	
11		11	

20 December
Sunday

2020

PRIORITY TASKS

TO DO

NOTES

	MORNING		AFTERNOON/EVENING
12 AM		12 PM	
1		1	
2		2	
3		3	
4		4	
5		5	
6		6	
7		7	
8		8	
9		9	
10		10	
11		11	

21 December Monday 2020

PRIORITY TASKS

_____
_____
_____
_____
_____
_____

TO DO

_____
_____
_____
_____
_____
_____
_____

NOTES

	MORNING		AFTERNOON/EVENING
12 AM		12 PM	
1		1	
2		2	
3		3	
4		4	
5		5	
6		6	
7		7	
8		8	
9		9	
10		10	
11		11	

_____
_____
_____
_____

22 December
Tuesday
2020

PRIORITY TASKS

_____
_____
_____
_____
_____
_____
_____

TO DO

_____
_____
_____
_____
_____
_____
_____

NOTES

	MORNING		AFTERNOON/EVENING
12 AM		12 PM	
1		1	
2		2	
3		3	
4		4	
5		5	
6		6	
7		7	
8		8	
9		9	
10		10	
11		11	

_____
_____
_____

23 December Wednesday 2020

PRIORITY TASKS

_____
_____
_____
_____
_____
_____
_____

TO DO

_____
_____
_____
_____
_____
_____

NOTES

MORNING

12 AM		12 PM	
1		1	
2		2	
3		3	
4		4	
5		5	
6		6	
7		7	
8		8	
9		9	
10		10	
11		11	

AFTERNOON/EVENING

_____
_____
_____
_____

24 December Thursday 2020

PRIORITY TASKS

_____
_____
_____
_____
_____
_____
_____

TO DO

_____
_____
_____
_____
_____
_____
_____

NOTES

MORNING		AFTERNOON/EVENING	
12 AM		12 PM	
1		1	
2		2	
3		3	
4		4	
5		5	
6		6	
7		7	
8		8	
9		9	
10		10	
11		11	

_____
_____
_____
_____

25 December Friday 2020

PRIORITY TASKS

_____
_____
_____
_____
_____
_____
_____

TO DO

_____
_____
_____
_____
_____
_____
_____
_____

NOTES

MORNING		AFTERNOON/EVENING	
12 AM		12 PM	
1		1	
2		2	
3		3	
4		4	
5		5	
6		6	
7		7	
8		8	
9		9	
10		10	
11		11	

_____
_____
_____
_____

26 December
Saturday
2020

PRIORITY TASKS

_____
_____
_____
_____
_____
_____

TO DO

_____
_____
_____
_____
_____
_____

NOTES

MORNING		AFTERNOON/EVENING	
12 AM		12 PM	
1		1	
2		2	
3		3	
4		4	
5		5	
6		6	
7		7	
8		8	
9		9	
10		10	
11		11	

_____
_____
_____
_____

27 December
Sunday

2020

PRIORITY TASKS

_____
_____
_____
_____
_____
_____
_____
_____

TO DO

_____
_____
_____
_____
_____
_____
_____

NOTES

MORNING		**AFTERNOON/EVENING**	
12 AM		12 PM	
1		1	
2		2	
3		3	
4		4	
5		5	
6		6	
7		7	
8		8	
9		9	
10		10	
11		11	

_____
_____
_____
_____

28 December
Monday
2020

PRIORITY TASKS

MORNING

AFTERNOON/EVENING

12 AM		12 PM	
1		1	
2		2	
3		3	
4		4	
5		5	
6		6	
7		7	
8		8	
9		9	
10		10	
11		11	

TO DO

NOTES

29 December Tuesday 2020

PRIORITY TASKS

_____
_____
_____
_____
_____
_____
_____
_____

TO DO

_____
_____
_____
_____
_____
_____
_____

NOTES

MORNING		AFTERNOON/EVENING
12 AM		12 PM
1		1
2		2
3		3
4		4
5		5
6		6
7		7
8		8
9		9
10		10
11		11

_____
_____
_____
_____

30 December
Wednesday 2020

PRIORITY TASKS

_____
_____
_____
_____
_____
_____
_____
_____

TO DO

_____
_____
_____
_____
_____
_____
_____
_____

NOTES

MORNING		AFTERNOON/EVENING	
12 AM		12 PM	
1		1	
2		2	
3		3	
4		4	
5		5	
6		6	
7		7	
8		8	
9		9	
10		10	
11		11	

_____
_____
_____
_____

31 December
Thursday **2020**

PRIORITY TASKS

TO DO

NOTES

MORNING		AFTERNOON/EVENING
12 AM		12 PM
1		1
2		2
3		3
4		4
5		5
6		6
7		7
8		8
9		9
10		10
11		11